GIVE

FIRST

GIVE

THE POWER
OF MENTORSHIP

FIRST

BRAD FELD

IDEAPRESS
PUBLISHING

WASHINGTON, DC

IDEAPRESS
PUBLISHING

Ideapress Publishing | www.ideapresspublishing.com

All trademarks are the property of their respective companies.

Cover Design: Faceout Studio, Spencer Fuller
Interior Design: Jessica Angerstein
Author Photo: The Scobeys

Cataloging-in-Publication Data is on file with the Library of Congress.

ISBN: 978-1-64687-132-2

Special Sales
Ideapress books are available at a special discount for bulk purchases for sales promotions and premiums or for use in corporate training programs. Special editions, including personalized covers, custom forewords, corporate imprints, and bonus content, are also available.

1 2 3 4 5 6 7 8 9 10

To two of my peer mentors:

Len Fassler, whom I think of and miss every day, for
providing the elemental fire that forged my philosophy about
how to behave in business relationships,

and

David Cohen, who inspires me with the energy he puts
into founders all over the world.

Contents

PART 3: NAVIGATING GIVE FIRST

PART 4: ENTREPRENEURIAL TZEDAKAH

PART 1

GIVE
FIRST

The Moment

It was the summer of 2001, and Interliant, a public company I had co-founded, was falling apart. I sat at the breakfast table at Len Fassler's house in Harrison, New York.

I was exhausted. Len and I co-founded Interliant with Steve Maggs and Rajat Bhargava in 1996 and took the company public in 1999. At its peak, it was worth around $3 billion. I was also a partner at Mobius Venture Capital and sat on over 25 boards, including five non-US companies and three other public company boards. If you multiplied the stock prices of each of the four public companies, you ended up with a smaller number than any of their individual stock prices.[1]

I was chewing on a bagel and sipping on a cup of coffee while staring out of Len's kitchen window, wondering what new version of a fucked-up shitstorm I was about to experience during the long day that would unfold. By this point, I had accepted that each day would be worse than the preceding one. Instead of going to bed hoping the next day would be better, I woke up each morning wondering what new difficulties the day would bring.

I no longer remember why I was at Len's house that day, but I often stayed there while visiting Interliant's headquarters in Purchase, New York. I do remember that the coffee was hot.

Len walked in with a bounce in his step like he did every time I saw him. He stopped, looked at me, and asked, "What's wrong?"

---

1 Each stock traded for less than $1 at the time. The companies were Interliant, MessageMedia, PeoplePC, and Raindance.

I looked up at him and said, "I'm tired. I didn't sleep well last night. I know today is going to suck. I don't feel like I can catch a break."

He looked at me, walked over slowly, stood behind me, put his hands on my shoulders, and said, "Suit up. They can't kill you, and they can't eat you. We'll get through it."

He patted me on the back and went to get a cup of coffee. I sat silently for a moment, stood up, turned around, and smiled at Len.

"Thanks," I said from the bottom of my heart.

He hugged me.

Len had an incredibly successful business career. He didn't have to co-found Interliant with Steve, me, and Rajat, and he didn't have to get up daily to go to the office, but he did it anyway—and he did it with a smile.

I first met Len in the spring of 1993, when I was 28 and he was 60. I quickly noticed that almost everyone around him loved him. While an outstanding negotiator, he exuded a graceful ease and was known as someone who always lived up to his word. He was consistently generous, always going out of his way to ensure the people around him felt part of whatever he was involved in. When he was with you, he was really with you. Occasionally, he'd get angry or frustrated, but he woke up each morning with a clean slate. Periodically, someone didn't fall head over heels for him, but the number of people who would follow him anywhere, do anything for him, and work tirelessly for whatever he was involved in was endless.

I became one of them.

At that moment in Len's kitchen, I realized why this was true. Len was someone who always gave more than he received. The energy he put into me and his relationship with me far exceeded any expectations

I might have had when he bought my company, Feld Technologies, eight years earlier. I immediately felt a connection with him and his partner, Jerry Poch. As time passed, I felt loyal to Jerry, and he taught me to address contentious or challenging issues head-on. But I truly loved Len. I loved him for his style, how he made people feel, and for his willingness to work through anything.

I felt guilty about dragging Len into the mess that had become Interliant. But, when I'd mention this to him, he'd tell me to let it go since it was his choice to get involved.

With each passing month, the mess got worse. Finally, when the Internet bubble began to deflate and ultimately burst, we knew we needed to quickly reach profitability since it was unlikely we'd be able to raise more money anytime soon. Three layoffs later, our CEO suddenly quit. Our stock price declined every week, feeling like it was losing 10 percent of whatever the previous value was the prior week, on a relentless march toward zero. There wasn't a clear path forward in the rare moments when I could pause and reflect.

Yet, there wasn't a single day that Len didn't give it his all.

After the hug, we got in his car to drive to our headquarters. The ever-present smell of cigars that Len smoked on walks at the end of the day was in the air. I didn't realize it yet, but that morning fundamentally shaped how I would think about the rest of my working life.

Len's statement, "They can't kill you, and they can't eat you," would echo in my mind repeatedly. It's just business. Even if the company fails, people will remember you for how you behaved and treated others in difficult situations. They can't kill you. You'll survive. They can't eat you. You'll still be around after it's over, regardless of what happens to the company.

A Definition

"Give First" means being willing to put energy into a relationship or a system without defining the transactional parameters. However, it's not altruism. You can and should expect to get something back. But you don't know when, from whom, in what form, or over what time frame.

How This Book Is Organized

While this book primarily focuses on mentorship, the concept of Give First encompasses a philosophy of behavior. However, after writing many words in an early draft, I decided that a book on the philosophy of behavior in an entrepreneurial context wasn't interesting. One day, I was looking up the Techstars Mentor Manifesto to send to someone and decided I wanted to build a book around it to explain the philosophy of Give First.

In 2006, David Cohen, David Brown, Jared Polis, and I co-founded Techstars in Boulder, Colorado. It started as an experiment as an alternative to angel investing, where we'd fund 10 companies at a time, work closely with them for 90 days, and surround them with other entrepreneurs and investors to help them rapidly iterate on their initial idea.

By 2011, Techstars had invested in over 100 companies, expanded to four cities (Boulder, Boston, Seattle, and New York), and the founders had interacted with hundreds of mentors. David Cohen published his observations of which mentor behaviors helped founders and what it meant to be a great mentor, calling this document the Techstars Mentor Manifesto.

This book brings together three concepts.

1. Mentorship at Techstars and its implementation
2. How mentorship fits with the Give First philosophy
3. Stories from my work that show the power of this philosophy in action

PART 1 explains the philosophy of Give First and where it came from.

PART 2 uses the Techstars Mentor Manifesto to explore how mentoring in an entrepreneurial context works. Each chapter has three parts: the explanation of the item of the Techstars Mentor Manifesto, how it fits with Give First, and an example. Many of the examples are autobiographical. While some of my examples are not from Techstars, each applies to the particular item at some level.

PART 3 explores navigating Give First. As with any philosophy, Give First has many challenges. I'll describe some of them and offer approaches to address or mitigate these challenges.

PART 4 talks about a concept I call Entrepreneurial Tzedakah. The word *tzedakah* is Hebrew for "righteousness" or "justice" and is commonly used to refer to charity or a good deed. While Give First isn't philanthropy, many philanthropic activities support entrepreneurship and conform nicely to the Give First philosophy. As examples, I'll describe two organizations I've been involved in co-founding: The Entrepreneurs Foundation of Colorado (which evolved into Pledge 1% Colorado and ultimately into Pledge 1%) and the Techstars Foundation.

The Origin

In 2012, when I was writing *Startup Communities: Building an Entrepreneurial Ecosystem in Your City*, the concept of Give First wove its way into many ideas in the book. At the time, I referred to it as "Give Before You Get," which I described as:

> One of my deeply held beliefs to the secret of success in life is to give before you get. In this approach, I am always willing to try to be helpful to anyone, without having a clear expectation of what is in it for me. If, over time, the relationship is one way (e.g., I'm giving, but getting nothing), I'll often back off on my level of give because this belief doesn't underlie a fundamentally altruistic approach. However, by investing time and energy up front without a specifically defined outcome, I have found that, over time, the rewards that come back to me exceed my wildest expectations.

A few decades ago, a group of founders worked hard to incorporate this Give Before You Get philosophy into the Boulder startup community. You rarely hear the words, "What's in it for me?" around Boulder; instead, it's "How can I be helpful?" While we were figuring it out as we went along, by the time *Startup Communities* came out, Give Before You Get was a foundational behavioral characteristic of the startup community in Boulder.

Techstars started in Boulder in 2006 and was one of the organizations amplifying the concept. From the beginning, Techstars incorporated mentors and mentorship deeply into the program, and we referred to Techstars as a "mentor-driven accelerator."

We defined a vital attribute of a Techstars mentor as someone willing to contribute time and energy to a mentee without expecting anything specific in return. David Cohen talks about this idea constantly and leads by example, not just with Techstars companies but also with many other companies where he's not an investor. Programs like Techstars Startup Weekend help founders at the beginning of their entrepreneurial journey get involved in startups and their startup community. If you ask Techstars mentors why they participate, many say, "Someone once helped me when I was a young founder; I want to give back."

But giving back is not enough. In 2011, Will Herman, a close friend (we made our first angel investment together back in 1994) and mentor at Techstars from the beginning, had a long discussion with Katie Rae, then the managing director of Techstars Boston. Katie asked Will why he mentored. Will doesn't remember his response, but Katie said, "Oh, you want to give back." Will said, "No, that's not right. To give back, you had to receive first." He then explained that he had never had an entrepreneurial mentor and wanted to make the path easier for others. Will's explanation was one of the earliest distinctions I remember between "giving back" and "giving first."

In 2013, after I published *Startup Communities*, Adam Grant published *Give and Take: Why Helping Others Drives Our Success*. I didn't know Adam then, but I connected to him through a friend and talked to him about my Give Before You Get idea. It was a delightful moment of simpatico for me as Adam got it and had done extensive research validating the concept before I even knew it was an idea.

One day in 2014, I noticed that my friends at Techstars had started tagging things on Twitter that were examples of Give Before You Get with #GiveFirst. Gregg Cochran, the Techstars Director of Implementation, spoke about the idea at a Techstars NYC mentor event, where several mentors started tweeting #GiveFirst. Gregg told David about it, who said, "Let's put it everywhere!"

So they did. And "Give First" was born.

My Earlier Experiences

Between 1983 and 1995, I lived in Cambridge and Boston, where I had my first experiences with entrepreneurship and startup communities.

I co-founded my first successful company, Feld Technologies, with Dave Jilk, in 1987, after earlier fledgling efforts withered. We only knew one other founder, Will Herman, with whom Dave had previously worked. Dave and I periodically hung out with Will, but beyond that, I felt pretty alone around entrepreneurship.

In 1991, I participated in the inaugural Birthing of Giants event. It was a four-day experience for founders (60 of them) created by Verne Harnish in conjunction with *Inc. Magazine* and hosted at MIT's Endicott House. It was the first time I had spent extended time with other founders, and it was a transformational experience.

I learned about YEO (the Young Entrepreneurs' Organization) at Birthing of Giants and quickly co-founded the Boston Chapter. YEO was a younger cousin to YPO (Young Presidents' Organization), with the membership requirements of being a founder—under 40 years old—of a company with at least $1 million in annual revenue. We quickly grew the Boston YEO chapter to 30 members, and I joined the board of YEO International. Suddenly, I was surrounded by other founders.

AmeriData, which Len Fassler and Jerry Poch ran, acquired Feld Technologies in 1993. Of my peers, I was one of the first founders to have a company acquired. While working for AmeriData, I started making angel investments. I got involved in helping start the MIT

Entrepreneurship Center. I spent time with my founder friends, helping them with their companies. I started working with Jana Matthews and the Kauffman Foundation on a new initiative called "Learning Programs for High Growth Companies."

This experience was all-consuming and delightful. In 1995, I stopped working full time for AmeriData and started a new company called Intensity Ventures. My network expanded quickly, and I found myself in the middle of the inception of the rise of the commercial Internet. My 100-hour weeks as a founder shifted into 100-hour weeks as a founder, investor, and advisor. It was a blast but often overwhelming and exhausting.

I learned how to structure my time more effectively but continued to engage broadly with anyone who reached out to me. I abandoned creating a hierarchy around me, preferring to work directly with everyone. However, I prioritized different relationships other than my personal ones, which would haunt me around 2001. I discuss this experience extensively in *Startup Life: Surviving and Thriving in a Relationship with an Entrepreneur,* which my wife, Amy Batchelor, and I published in 2013.

In 1995, Amy and I moved to Boulder. While I stayed connected to Boston, I shifted my energy to my new home, leveraging the formidable experience I'd had in Boston around building a startup community and incorporating the behavior I learned from that experience, which evolved into the philosophy of Give First.

What Give First Isn't

Whenever I talk about Give First, especially when building startup communities, the phrase "Pay It Forward" comes up. Often, someone asks me, "How is Give First different from Paying It Forward?"

While these concepts are cousins, Paying It Forward is obligatory and transactional. You pay it forward because once, earlier in your career, someone did something for you. Now, you are paying it forward to someone else by helping them. You aren't doing this as a continuous part of your way of being. Instead, it is an obligation due to something that someone else did for you.

Although you can pay it forward at any point, talking about this as a later-in-life event is common. You can pay it forward over and over again, but it's more typical to link paying it forward to a single event or experience. And, even though paying it forward can create a feedback loop, it usually describes a one-directional set of behaviors.

Paying It Forward is fantastic but it is limited. In contrast, Give First is a mindset that invites you to be helpful before someone has done something for you. I felt we needed a different phrase and concept to break out of a transactional mindset and reinforce the positive feedback loops that can impact an entire community rather than just an individual.

The Power of Give First

Even the origin story of Techstars embodies the idea of Give First. While neither David Cohen nor I realized it then, our initial interaction set the tone for what has become a fundamental philosophy of Techstars.

In 2006, I was well known in Colorado as an early-stage investor. An endless stream of people wanted to meet with me. While I liked to be broadly available, I was chronically overscheduled, harried, and overwhelmed when I tried to squeeze in these short introductory meetings between the other stuff I was doing. Eventually, I separated these introductory meetings into a dedicated Random Day. Once a month, I'd do 10 to 20 back-to-back meetings, each 15 minutes long, and get together with anyone who wanted to meet.

I didn't know David, but he got on my Random Day calendar, and three months later, we sat down to talk for 15 minutes. I didn't recognize him, but he knew me from my reputation, a few shared friends, and a company named Solidware, in which we were both angel investors.

He slid a homemade brochure across the table. At the top, it featured an early version of the Techstars logo. The brochure described a "three-month mentorship and investment program for startups." I skimmed it while he explained the idea. He was nervous and soft-spoken, so I stopped reading, made eye contact, and concentrated on listening to him.

David told me he had previously co-founded, built, and sold Pinpoint Technologies with his business partner, David Brown. While Pinpoint was about 10 minutes from my office, I'd never heard of it. David said he'd started making angel investments with some of the money he'd made from the sale but wasn't enjoying it because it felt random and unfulfilling. He wanted to be more helpful and engaged with the founders of the companies he invested in.

David had a concept that we eventually started calling an "accelerator," which would fund 10 new companies each summer, surround them with intensive mentorship from the Boulder community, and provide a small amount of investment capital to each company in exchange for equity.

I instantly loved this idea. My previous venture capital firm, Mobius Venture Capital, was no longer making investments, and we hadn't yet started raising money for my current firm, Foundry's, first fund. At the time, I was making about one angel investment a month, using a similar strategy to the one I used when I started making angel investments in 1994. While I was a very visible angel investor, I empathized with David's frustration, especially since, in 2006, seed and early-stage investing in tech companies was still out of favor.

David told me he wanted to raise a modest amount of money. He was willing to contribute about a third of it and thought David Brown would contribute something, but he was looking for a few other people to join him.

I said, "I'm in for as long as you aren't a flake or a crook, and I can figure that out quickly." While surprised, David kept a good poker face and said, "That's great. Do you know anyone else who might be interested?"

We were about 10 minutes into our 15-minute random meeting when I asked David to sit tight for a minute. I then stepped out of the conference room and called my longtime friend Jared Polis, who had several entrepreneurial successes, including BlueMountainArts.com and Provide Commerce. Jared answered.

"Jared. It's Brad Feld. I just committed to investing in a new thing called Techstars, which I want to talk to you about and see if you are interested in investing with me."

"Count me in," he said. "What is it?"

I explained that an entrepreneur in Boulder named David Cohen created it to fund 10 new companies over the summer, work with them for 90 days, and see what happens. We discussed how this could be a cool way to get more startups funded and up and running in Boulder while connecting them to some founders and investors.

I returned to the room and said Jared and I would fill in the rest of the round. David and I smiled. The 15 minutes were up, so we ended the meeting.

Just like that, Techstars was funded. Without my Random Day, I might never have met David in this context. My willingness, and Jared's, to invest quickly, without knowing where this would or could go, generated magic.

We were motivated by the potential impact the experiment could have on Boulder. At the time, the phrases "startup community" and "give first" didn't exist, but with hindsight, we were giving first to the Boulder startup community.

We never imagined this would turn into a company that funded over 4,000 companies worldwide and impacted hundreds of thousands of founders. Instead, we were excited to engage without knowing what we'd get back.

PART 2

MENTORING

The Beginning

When we started Techstars in 2006, the concept of a mentor was fuzzy. Many people and organizations called themselves "advisors" to startups, including the entire pantheon of service providers. While the word *mentor* existed, it was usually a one-to-one relationship and more prevalent in corporate America, where to make your way up the corporate ladder, you needed a "mentor," "sponsor," or a "rabbi."

We used the word mentor to describe the relationship between the Boulder startup community participants and the founders who went through Techstars. Our first program had about 50 mentors. Many were local Boulder founders, a few were service providers who were particularly active in the startup community, several were investors, and the rest were non-Boulder founders and VCs. To recruit them, I contacted a bunch of my friends and asked, "Would you be a mentor for this new Techstars thing we are doing?" Most quickly said yes.

In 2006, we had no real clue about the relationship between a mentor and a founder. The idea of an accelerator was still in the invention phase, and the concept of a "mentor-driven accelerator" didn't exist. However, we knew we wanted real engagement from the mentors rather than just a list of advisors on a website. We expected that engaging local mentors would be easier than non-local mentors. We defined rules of engagement around what mentoring meant, which did not preclude early investment but prohibited charging any fees during the accelerator program.

As mentorship became popular, everyone suddenly wanted to be a mentor, and there was an overwhelming supply. In 2008, we began to understand what was effective and what wasn't. While we tried to include anyone who wanted to be a mentor, many people simply spent a day with the accelerator program, meeting with each company but never engaging meaningfully with any individual founder.

In 2011, we began putting structure around mentorship. By then, the phrase "mentor" had entered trendy language land, and everyone was calling themselves a mentor, even if they weren't. Being a Techstars mentor suddenly appeared as a job title on people's LinkedIn bios.[2]

By this point, we were starting to understand effective mentorship.

---

2 Today, over 20,000 people list Techstars on their LinkedIn bio. See https://www.linkedin.com/search/results/people/?keywords=techstars.

The Techstars Mentor Manifesto

In August 2011, David Cohen published the Techstars Mentor Manifesto. We had run 11 Techstars accelerator programs in four cities, totaling 110 companies. We worked with over 200 mentors. Each program was managed by a different managing director, however, so the mentor dynamics, while compelling, were inconsistent.

As we received more requests to provide structure around mentoring and "mentor training," David, with help from Jon Bradford (who became the Techstars London Managing Director) and I, came up with 18 bullet points.[3]

1. Be Socratic.

2. Expect nothing in return (you'll be delighted with what you do get back).

3. Be authentic—practice what you preach.

4. Be direct. Tell the truth, however hard.

5. Listen, too.

6. The best mentor relationships eventually become two-way.

7. Be responsive.

8. Adopt at least one company every single year. Experience counts.

9. Clearly separate opinion from fact.

---

3 "The Mentor Manifesto," David Cohen, August 28, 2011, https://davidgcohen. com/2011/08/28/the-mentor-manifesto/.

10. Hold information in confidence.

11. Clearly commit to mentor or do not. Either is fine.

12. Know what you don't know. Say "I don't know" when you don't know. "I don't know" is preferable to bravado.

13. Guide, don't control. Teams must make their own decisions. Guide, but never tell them what to do. Understand that it's their company, not yours.

14. Accept and communicate with other mentors that get involved.

15. Be optimistic.

16. Provide specific actionable advice; don't be vague.

17. Be challenging/robust but never destructive.

18. Have empathy. Remember that startups are hard.

The Difference between Mentors, Advisors, and Investors

During the first year of Techstars, we established that mentoring was a non-compensated activity. Occasionally, someone would explicitly ask for compensation before agreeing to be a mentor. We didn't yet have language around Give First, so we'd try to explain the indirect and non-financial benefits of being involved in Techstars as a mentor. We'd introduce the person to another mentor to hear about their experiences as a Techstars mentor. Usually, this helped, but sometimes it didn't.

We quickly understood the difference between an advisor and a mentor. An advisor says, "I'll help you if you give me a $3,000/month retainer and 1 percent of your company." A mentor says, "How can I help?"

We had a similar experience with investors. Many were interested in being mentors just to be close to the companies. Some looked for something special, usually unique access to the companies. A few would ask for an economic benefit, such as a warrant or an opportunity to invest at a low price, even if the company wasn't raising money. Whenever this came up, we'd explain the benefits of being involved as a mentor well before demo day without any specific contractual obligations.

When the person got it and understood Give First, even if we didn't have the words for it, they were often a great mentor. When they didn't, we were polite and ensured they were on the various Techstars mailing lists, but we didn't invite them to continue being a mentor in the program.

Our goal was not to be anti-advisor, as advisors have a clear role in the world. Instead, we were trying to define a new helper category for founders and provide a clear and consistent framework for a mentor's behavior in a company's early stages.

As companies raise money, mentors often become investors in the company. Sometimes, they became compensated advisors, especially mentors with professional coaching businesses. This evolution is natural, but a non-compensated mentor relationship is ideal at the earliest stages of a company.

Mentorship Is One-to-One, not One-to-Many

In the first year, Techstar's mentors were mainly my friends. About half lived in Boulder and Denver, but the other half lived in California, New York, and Boston. My network was national since I'd invested across the US since the mid-1990s. We chose the mentors thoughtfully, trying to get people involved who would do more than show up in Boulder for a day.

When someone came to town, they weren't only making a trip to give a talk to a group of 30 founders eager to listen. Sure, they wanted to spend some time with me, and I wanted to spend some time with them, but they wanted to get to know the founders. During the day, they'd have 10 meetings that lasted 30 minutes each, with a break for a group lunch. While they'd meet with each team and discuss what each company was doing, the focus was often on the founders.

During the day, the out-of-town mentor would give a talk to the entire group. Sometimes, this was their personal entrepreneurial story. Sometimes, it was about a specific thing their company was doing that might be helpful to the companies. Sometimes, it was an AMA.

It was a long day for the mentor. If they stayed overnight, David and I often took them out to dinner. Sometimes, they'd stay another day and visit some companies in Boulder, especially if they were investors or just wanted to better understand the Boulder scene. Often, they circled back to spend more time with several of the founders whom they were particularly interested in helping.

The idea that mentorship was one-to-one, mentor to founder, emerged from this.

As Techstars expanded to other cities, such as Boston, Seattle, and New York, I'd travel to each city several times during the accelerator program. I'd always try to spend one day at Techstars using this pattern. I'd meet with every company for 30 minutes but focus on the founders and how I could be helpful to them. I'd host a group event—often lunch or dinner. I frequently stayed in the city for several days because of other portfolio company commitments. I usually circled back to the accelerator for a little more time one-on-one with a few founders.

As other accelerators were created, such as Excelerate in Chicago and Springboard in London, I ran the same mentor drill there. In conversations about mentoring with David and my Foundry partners, we began to define mentorship as a one-to-one experience. While sitting in an audience and hearing a story or doing an AMA with an experienced person is interesting, there is something special about one-to-one mentorship.

While one-to-many interactions are much more efficient for the presenter, this isn't mentoring. It's a presentation. There are topics where one-to-many works great, and over the years at Techstars we've engaged hundreds of speakers across thousands of sessions designed in this way. However, this method doesn't develop a relationship between a mentor and a mentee. While it allows for questions, they are usually asked in the wrong direction (from the audience to the presenter) in the context of mentorship.

Deconstructing the Techstars Mentor Manifesto

In 2014, Nicole Glaros was the managing director of Techstars Boulder. She held a great Mentor Kickoff event at the Bohemian Biergarten, where she read the Techstars Mentor Manifesto. Nicole's performance inspired me to define mentorship and how a mentor can optimally interact with a startup, especially one at a very early stage or one consisting of first-time founders.

I wrote 18 blog posts,[4] each defining and describing each item in the Techstars Mentor Manifesto. Over the years, people encouraged me to turn these posts into a book. A similar thing happened with the blog posts that Jason Mendelson and I wrote in 2005 about term sheets—that ultimately became the starting point for our book *Venture Deals: Be Smarter Than Your Lawyer and Venture Capitalist*. The posts represent only a fraction of the following 18 chapters, but they got me started.

Each chapter has three sections. The first is the definition and detailed description of the item in the Techstars Mentor Manifesto. The second section contains additional thoughts about the item or something from my experience that complements or extends the concept. The last section is a story from my experience that relates to the item in some way, ranging from "precise" to "extremely loosely connected."

---

4   "Deconstructing the Mentor Manifesto," Brad Feld, July 9, 2014, https://feld.com/archives/2014/07/deconstructing-mentor-manifesto/.

Be Socratic

If you think "Be Socratic" means "ask questions," you are partially correct. When David crafted the mentor manifesto, he started with "Be Socratic" since asking questions is a crucial part of the Techstars mentor process. But it's not just the act of asking questions; it's how you ask the questions, what you try to accomplish with the questions, and your responses to the answers.

The "how" is essential. As a mentor, it's easy to establish a one-up–one-down relationship with a founder. In most cases, you start that way, especially with first-time founders. However, your goal should be to create a peer relationship where the mentee learns from the mentor, and equally importantly, the mentor learns from the mentee. This mutual learning is crucial to the process and makes the mentor feel valued. As a result, tone matters.

Begin by eliminating judgment from your questions. When you ask questions, keep them open-ended. For example, instead of "Is this customer important?" you could ask, "Who are the customers you are interested in?" Avoid yes-or-no questions so the mentee has room to answer. If they don't answer your direct question, listen to what they are saying and try to reformulate your question in a new way to get them to address it.

The cliché "there are no stupid questions" applies. Body language matters. If you—as the mentor—don't understand something, ask. You don't have to show the mentee you are more intelligent than them. You don't have to establish your credibility—you already have it.

Your credibility as a mentor is a crucial asset, and it should give you confidence in your role.

One of your goals with these questions is to learn more about the company and the problem you are exploring. However, if this becomes a one-way Q&A, your mentee will only be getting part of the value out of the experience. Try to use your questions to guide the discussion, presumably toward testing hypotheses. Lead with the questions while showing your thought process. This approach can be subtle, where you guide things along. Or, it can be explicit, where you state your hypothesis and start asking questions.

Instead of coming up with or stating the answer, help the mentee figure out the answer or a set of new hypotheses they can test. Your goal shouldn't be only to solve the immediate problem. Instead, you are helping your mentee build a toolset to solve future issues independently. This process is collaborative, especially if you are trying to develop a peer relationship. It won't happen comfortably in your first interaction. Still, after time together, you'll learn from each other and reach a better set of answers or at least new hypotheses to test.

The Five Whys

Often, the answer to a question isn't the root cause of the problem or even close. When this happens, ask, "Why?"

Use the Five Whys[5] methodology to get to the root cause of any issue.

---

5 "Five Whys," Wikipedia, accessed on March 20, 2025, https://en.wikipedia.org/wiki/Five_whys.

Let's use a non–tech industry example:

The vehicle will not start.

Why? The battery is dead.

Why? The alternator is not functioning.

Why? The alternator belt has broken.

Why? The alternator belt was well beyond its useful service life and not replaced.

Why? The vehicle was not maintained according to the recommended service schedule.

The first few answers are valid but do not address the root cause of the problem. Replacing the battery might solve a short-term problem but won't solve the longer-term issue. Even replacing the alternator belt doesn't address the root cause of the problem. If you don't maintain the vehicle according to the recommended service schedule, you will likely reencounter this problem.

Now, let's use a software example:

The website is slow.

Why? The server is overloaded.

Why? There are a large number of concurrent requests.

Why? There are a large number of new visitors to the site.

Why? A recent marketing campaign generates them, but the users aren't signing up.

Why? The marketing campaign was too broad and needs to be tuned.

What matters is the root cause. And that's what you are trying to get to with your questions. Don't dismiss the first answer. Keep digging. Use the third answer to set up several hypotheses because you are getting into the meat of the issue.

The goal is not to end up with the definitive answer to the questions but to create a new set of hypotheses to test. You are at the beginning of a long arc of inquisition. Be Socratic in a continuous process to find answers.

The Near Death of Simple Energy

In May 2015, Simple Energy, a Techstars 2011 company building energy-efficiency software for utilities, was in dire straits. The founders, Yoav Lurie and Justin Segall reached out to meet with me as part of the Blackstone Entrepreneurs Network (BEN) Colorado mentoring program, which I had co-founded in 2014.

I wasn't a direct investor in Simple Energy but an indirect investor via Techstars. I wasn't aware of what was happening with the company and hadn't talked to Yoav or Justin in at least six months. I didn't know why they wanted to meet with me, but I was happy to as part of the BEN Colorado mentoring program and Yoav and Justin's connection to Techstars.

They quickly updated me on their predicament. They had under a month of cash left in the bank, had just turned down a crummy acquisition offer, and were trying to figure out what to do.

After their last financing a year earlier, they had overhired, including adding several experienced but expensive executives, because their investors told them they needed to. They expanded too quickly, including launching in Europe before they had product-market fit in the US. Given the pressure to grow, they stopped living their values as founders. Consequently, they fell in love with vanity metrics such as headcount and weighted pipeline instead of revenue and profitability.

Yoav and Justin believed they could navigate through things since they had late-stage customer prospects worth at least $1 million in near-term revenue and cash flow that they thought they could close in August. They just needed to stay alive for the next three months.

They were living off debt from their venture lender and hadn't considered what would happen if the August money didn't show up— or even how to make it to August. I encouraged them to talk to their lawyer to understand the dynamics of debt vs. equity and meet with me on Monday morning to go deeper into the financial reality of where they were.

When we met, I used the Five Whys to investigate the root causes of how they got into this position, what needed to happen to make it past August, why they thought this could happen, and what would happen if it didn't.

After a lengthy discussion, we developed a short-term plan. I then asked Yoav and Justin another question: "What happens to the business on the other side of this plan, and is it worth it to reset where you are and start building from there?"

Several days later, they laid off 65 percent of the team and raised $1 million in convertible notes from their investors. They tore the poster with their "old values" off the wall and reset their new values to align with who they were. They started communicating extremely clearly with the entire team, mentors, and investors about their cash position and the core activities and metrics to build the company. They took a disciplined approach, starting with an email at 5 a.m. every Monday covering all aspects of the business, including metrics of each team, cash balance and forecast, and a letter from the CEO. This 5 a.m. email went out weekly for the next four years.

After almost dying in the spring of 2015, Simple Energy grew from $4 million in revenue in 2015 to $12 million in 2016, $25 million in 2017, and $45 million in 2018. They scaled the company without new equity but did find a new debt provider and used a debt facility to help them do so.

In 2018, they took on a strategic investment that included Yoav and Justin selling some of their stock at 10 times the price previously offered for their almost-dead business in 2015. They then led a five-company PE-backed rollup to create Uplight, which became the utility industry's leading customer engagement software platform. In 2021, Uplight was acquired for $1.5 billion.

Expect Nothing in Return

When you expect nothing in return, you will often be delighted with what you get. It's extraordinarily simple while profoundly challenging.

It's simple because it's easy to say, "I'm doing this without any expectations." That feels good, right? You will be a good mentor, helping another up-and-coming founder, and it'll be good karma. It's good marketing. Who doesn't like people to say things about her like, "Jill is so awesome. She helped me without expecting anything back." The satisfaction of helping others is a reward in itself.

It's also profoundly challenging because this isn't human nature, especially in business. We live in a transactional world, constantly deciding where to invest our time to get the best ROI. There's even a phrase for that—"return on invested time." We worry about reputational effects and are cautious about spending too much time with low-impact activities or unknown people while being drawn to the spotlight and well-known people, even if the activities are hollow and lack substance or value. We often feel overwhelmed with our base level of work and struggle to justify spending time on activities with an unknown impact. We prioritize how we spend our time, gravitating toward things where we can see the payoff.

Give First broke this cycle for me and became the essence of how I think about mentorship. Remember, Give First isn't altruism. You will get something back. You don't know when, from whom, in what currency, or in what magnitude. You enter the relationship non-transactionally and continue giving without a defined return. By expecting nothing in return, you enable yourself to Give First. This approach may not yield immediate results, but it can lead to long-term benefits and build a network of trust and goodwill that can be invaluable.

While trying to understand how startup communities worked, I realized that Give First helped resolve the bootstrap problem (also called the cold-start problem), which is about getting a new system or community started. To activate a startup community, you have to get everyone in the startup community to put energy into the community before they get any value back. They have to Give First, and if you can create a culture where everyone involved operates without any expectation of getting anything in return, magical things happen quickly as an enormous amount of energy goes into the system. This concept has the power to transform not only business relationships but also the entire entrepreneurial ecosystem, fostering a culture of collaboration and mutual support.

It's important to remember that this isn't altruism. You will get something back, but you don't have any expectations about what it will be.

Compensation

While there is no direct compensation for mentoring, a mentor can be compensated in many ways. The essence of this compensation lies in the non-transactional nature of the experience, where any outcome is a bonus to the mentoring experience.

At its core, mentoring is a profound learning experience. In my relationships with Len Fassler and David Cohen, we learned from each other. There was a moment when I knew Len felt like he was learning as much from me as I was learning from him. The feeling of being peers and learning from each other differed from the mentor-mentee dynamic and also happened in my relationship with David. Early on, I realized I was learning a lot just by being around him and watching him interact with others. The peer mentorship feedback loop kicked in when I listened to him more carefully.

Will Herman told me that listening is the only thing he expects from a mentee.[6] After noticing many meetings were check-the-box activities, where the founder felt obligated to meet with the mentor, Will began telling the founders, "You never need to take any of my advice. But my only expectation is that you listen to me and understand what I'm trying to say. That's my full expectation, and that's the only return I'm looking for." It's similar to what I regularly say: "What I'm saying is simply data for you. As long as you listen to and consider what I'm saying, I support any decision you make."

I have an extremely long list of people I'd now consider peer mentors who probably viewed me as a mentor at one point. Many of them likely don't even know I consider them mentors. I've learned more from many founders than they've learned from me. Some investors who have surpassed me in achievements and experience, and whom I regularly learn from when we interact, consider me a mentor. If you value learning, mentorship provides an endless source of it.

People don't have to be labeled mentors. While this is how it works in Techstars, where people sign up to be mentors and companies get matched with mentors, it doesn't have to be this way. You can mentor someone without their asking, and they can ask you for help without you being an official mentor. When someone asks me to be a mentor,

---

6   Will and Rajat Bhargava wrote a fantastic book, *The Startup Playbook*, which can be found at https://startup-playbook.com/.

I say, "There is no need for a formal relationship. Just ask me about anything at any time."

Economic opportunities emerge over time. As early-stage companies raise money, they often fundraise from their mentors. If you are a visible angel investor or early-stage VC, a founder will usually ask you to invest, but if you've also been a mentor, you'll have had lots of time to work with the founders to evaluate if you want to be an investor. Your mentorship has been your due diligence. If you are the founders' best mentor and early investor, it will be logical for them to ask you to be a board member and become even more involved.

If you view entrepreneurship as a multi-turn game, the experience of mentoring a founder is the start of a long-term relationship. The compensation, beyond learning, may not come from that first company. But, by playing a long-term, multi-turn game, you'll have many opportunities to be compensated for future things you do with the founder.

My Early Advisor/Mentor Experience

I sold Feld Technologies to AmeriData in November 1993. While working for AmeriData, I started meeting with founders in the fall of 1994, when my role shifted from a management position to a staff role working for Len Fassler and Jerry Poch. In the fall of 1994, I made my first angel investment.

I stopped working full time for AmeriData in early 1995 but remained a consultant. By then, I was an active angel investor, making at least one investment a month. However, many startups, including those that weren't raising money, asked me to help, so I started advising some startups.

This advising consisted of a monthly retainer ranging from $1,000 to $5,000 per month and a small amount of equity (shares or options). For $1,000 per month, I'd immediately respond to any email and phone call. For $3,000 per month, I'd add on a weekly conference call. For $5,000 per month, I'd also spend a day a month in person at your office.

Before I knew it, I was making a lot of money. My only constraint was time.

Some of the founders I advised started to become unhappy with me. They would say, "I paid you $3,000 last month, and you didn't spend enough time with me," even though I did what I said I would. Or, "I called you on Saturday at 7 p.m., and you didn't call me back immediately. I need you to come to the office right now—my co-founder and I are having a meltdown."

Today, part of what I was doing might be called "coaching." But coaching wasn't a thing in the 1990s, so I called it advising. Most coaches set good boundaries. I didn't. I'd help anyone, respond to everyone, and try to fit everything in. While some founders paid me, others didn't. While my reputation of being available and helpful accelerated, time remained my most significant constraint. My advising business didn't scale.

It was also starting to suck. I wasn't enjoying the work. I had started a new company, which ultimately became Interliant. I was now on several boards from my angel investments and had begun working with SoftBank, a Japanese company that was an early investor in many emerging Internet companies. I was traveling constantly and was getting exhausted.

Something had to change.

One month, on the last day, as I sat down to create invoices for the next month, I decided to fire all my clients. I called each one and told them I was retiring from the paid advisory business. They didn't owe me any more money. They wouldn't be getting another bill from me. If they wanted their stock back, I'd give it back to them. But, I'd still be happy to answer phone calls and emails anytime, and if I had invested in their company, I'd join their board if they wanted me and be available in person periodically.

All of them told me to keep my stock. Several were annoyed with me but expressed it mainly as a disappointment. Most understood, and a few were relieved because they could see I wasn't happy with how I was working.

I continued to be a free advisor for many of them. In some cases, the stock I received for being an advisor or an early angel investor paid off significantly, and I made many times more than I would have if I had kept charging $1,000 to $5,000 monthly. I was much happier as I transitioned into the next phase of my business life, unexpectedly becoming a venture capitalist while co-founding several companies.

Be Authentic–Practice What You Preach

When I started blogging in 2004, the word of the moment was "transparency." Fred Wilson led the way, and I happily followed. When transparency became a cliché, authenticity found its way into entrepreneurial lingo and has become trendy.

It's not about stating that you are authentic. It's about *being* authentic all the time, in every way. Of course, you will make mistakes. When you do, own them, apologize, correct things, and begin again.

Being authentic is especially important as a mentor. The founders you mentor look up to you and immediately entrust you with responsibility, so your authenticity is crucial to maintaining this relationship.

It's easy to fall into the trap of "I'm doing this as a favor to the founder, so they have to put up with me." Wrong. You are setting an example for the founder. They are watching your every move. The pressure on you is high since your behavior will rub off on your mentees.

Your behavior can be as simple as being on time. If you emphasize the importance of shipping on time to the founder but are consistently 15 minutes late to meetings, that's not authentic. If you stress the importance of a personal voice on the company blog but have a marketing team handle your content for your VC firm, that's not authentic. If you have a public persona of being calm and constructive but then throw temper tantrums to get the attention of your mentees, you are just being a jerk.

Sometimes you will be late for a meeting. You have the infrastructure the founder doesn't. You'll get frustrated and lose your temper sometimes. But when you do, own it and apologize. Let the founder know when you are inconsistent in your behavior. When they realize it's okay to screw up, they'll understand the power of being authentic.

Embrace the tenet "practice what you preach," which is at the core of an authentic mentor-mentee relationship. As a mentor, you are modeling behavior. Do your words match your actions?

Nonsense Phrases Such as "I'm Value Added"

I'm amused when someone says, "I'm authentic," "I'm transparent," "I'm founder-friendly," or "I'm a value-added investor." Whenever I hear something like that, I automatically insert the word "not" between "I'm" and the rest of the phrase.

I'm suspicious whenever someone says, "I'm an (adjective) (noun)." Why did you need to say, "I'm a great tennis player," "I'm a deep thinker," or "I'm a generous person"? Instead, why not simply play tennis, regardless of how great you are? Or think as deeply as you want? Or be generous?

In the world of venture capital, the phrases "value-added" and "founder-friendly" come up repeatedly. While the price of admission in VC is to provide money, almost every VC I know aspires to add value to their investments and support founders. Many don't add value or support founders, yet declare it loudly and regularly. Some investors even add negative value.

There's no need to say that you add value. Just do it. And, if you say you are value-added, consider if you are.

Being Full of Value-Added Shit

"Hmm," I thought to myself.

I had just watched a video interview with a famous VC. Although I didn't know him, I was friendly with several founders who had worked with him and knew of at least one of the situations he had described.

The VC's verbal fillers took up the first 30 minutes of the interview. There were plenty of "Honestly" and "To tell you the truth" woven in between "I'll be transparent about what happened" and "The best founders are authentic to their true selves."

One of his stories, which I was familiar with, didn't feel right. I knew the founder/CEO of the company he described and thought she'd had a particularly rough time with this VC. However, the VC's preamble was, "In difficult situations, I'm always transparent about what will happen with the founder. That way, they have an opportunity to challenge or correct me."

I emailed my founder-CEO friend to ask about the situation. I told her I'd just seen an interview with the VC in which he discussed her company. Had she seen the interview? Did she agree with what the VC said?

"He's full of shit," said my friend. "That guy is a manipulative psychopath. Before we even talked about the situation, he'd gone around me to everyone on my management team and planted seeds of doubt with them. He told different things to each team member, lied about our situation, and attributed things to me that hadn't happened at all."

"So, he wasn't transparent with you?"

"Are you kidding me? I have no idea why anyone takes this guy seriously."

"Did you when you first met him?"

"Well, yes, of course. He was charismatic, had a lot of capital, talked a good game, and had a lot of people who said great things about him."

"What do you think happened?"

"I think he's a manipulative, misogynistic, ego-challenged person who is deeply deceitful. Well, maybe he's not misogynistic, but all the people who liked him were men, and I've subsequently met a few other female founders who had similar experiences to mine."

The VC was neither transparent nor authentic. As is often the case, his reputation eventually caught up with him.

Be Direct. Tell the Truth, However Hard

At some level, being direct is easy. You say what is on your mind, lead with a clear statement, and support it with examples.

Many people find it difficult to be direct. They can't seem to get to the point. They thrive on inductive reasoning and are passive-aggressive, especially when they don't know the answer or are uncomfortable with the truth.

Consider how you answer a question when you don't know the answer. Do you use the powerful phrase "I don't know"? Or do you skirt around the question, searching for a somewhat relevant answer while reframing the question more to your liking? Or do you spew out whatever comes to mind, extrapolating truth from one data point lurking deep in your brain?

Don't do this.

Telling the truth is more complicated than being direct. I try hard not to lie. As a kid, I'd stretch the truth to exaggerate my self-importance or the perceived excitement of a story. I did a few things I was ashamed of and lied to cover them up and avoid exposing what I'd done. But I felt terrible about myself whenever I got caught in a lie. My parents handled this well, and instead of punishing me, they would talk about the deceit and make me face it. They were calm but direct and unyielding. At some point, I realized dealing with the ramifications of getting caught in a lie was much worse than telling the truth in the first place. And, if you tell the truth, you don't have to remember what to say. I thank my parents for instilling this value in me.

If you don't know the answer, say you don't know. But if you know, be direct. Be more than a cheerleader. While being optimistic is essential, when you aren't direct, the mentee loses an opportunity to hear challenging feedback. Cheerleading isn't lying but often glosses over the tough stuff.

The Cost of Passive Avoidance

Recently, the concept of "the truth" has become elusive. While mistruths, lies, and deceit have been a foundational part of our species' communication, a new level of misdirection and deflection around being direct and telling the truth became popular when the phrase "fake news" became part of our vocabulary.

In entrepreneurship, passive avoidance is a pernicious version of avoiding the truth. Every crisis communication playbook has a chapter on ignoring the crisis and pretending it's not happening. This approach is related to deflection, another deeply destructive maneuver from the crisis communication playbook, which follows another strategy: attack.

There are moments when I'm too tired or frustrated to deal with a situation. Or, I disagree with a path a team is going down, but I have other things on my mind, and I don't feel like bothering with it. Or I'm tired of arguing with someone, don't care anymore, or feel defeatist about the situation. That's passive-avoidant.

Reflecting on my past, I often regret when I was passive-avoidant. Many of my disappointments can be linked directly to being passive-avoidant. When Amy challenges me about something at work, it's usually about me being passive-avoidant. I feel anxiety when I'm avoiding dealing with something. And, when I look back at some of my depressive episodes, they often were triggered by an accumulation of avoiding things, including my own physical and emotional health, that I let build up until I couldn't handle it anymore.

If you realize you are acting passive-avoidant, pause and consider why you have fallen into this behavioral trap. Step back and get to the root cause of what is bothering you. Apply the Five Whys to the situation. Once you discover the root cause, decide if you should take action to address it. Or, should you disengage? Either way, you are now ready to be direct about what you are thinking, feeling, and going to do.

Passive-avoidant behavior is occasionally inevitable. But if you do it repeatedly, it builds up. You start being unable to confront situations. You begin avoiding being direct. Consequently, the other person doesn't hear challenging information that could impact their behavior. You stop telling the truth and get caught up in your deceit around a situation. You withdraw, where silence can do as much damage as hostility and attack.

Young Adult Lessons from Lying and Being Lied To

As a young adult, I exaggerated the truth but rarely purposefully lied. After my parents, my first business partner, Dave Jilk, was next to confront me about this behavior.

I was the primary salesperson at Feld Technologies, although Dave sold plenty of business over the years, especially with existing customers. Dave often got frustrated with me when I oversold something, which resulted in us starting a new client relationship with expectations that were far beyond what we could deliver. He got even more frustrated with me when I was selling him on my position, trying to convince him of something by stretching the truth, exaggerating the wonderfulness of the potential outcome, or just trying to push through an issue with the force of my personality.

Dave regularly challenged and pushed back on me, which eventually helped me realize that overselling, exaggerating, and overstating the situation ultimately lowered my credibility. When things built up, we knew how to de-escalate, which often involved dinner at Nara, a sushi restaurant around the corner from our office in Boston. Whenever Dave said, "Let's go get dinner at Nara," I knew something was up. He was always direct and never passive-avoidant.

That doesn't mean that I don't make mistakes. I make a lot of them—all the time. But I try not to shade the truth or outright lie. And when I do, and I realize it, I own it, which is another version of telling the truth. It's easy to gloss over the fact that you made a mistake. But it's much more powerful to own and correct your mistakes.

Listen, Too

Do you talk too much? I do. It's one of my weaknesses. I often try to make my point by giving examples and telling stories. I'm not afraid to be wrong, so I'll toss out an idea and discuss it. I don't go so far as to "think out loud" like some people, but I regularly talk too much and have to ratchet it back to listen consciously.

While mentorship begins with being Socratic, it's easy to fall into the trap of asking questions and quickly giving answers. Many people don't listen carefully, as they are already thinking about the next question, especially when the answer is vague or fuzzy. Moving on to the next question is easier than getting to the issue's root cause.

The next time you ask a question, empty your mind after the question and listen to the answer. Look directly into the eyes of the person you are with and concentrate on what they are saying. Don't move on to the next question or respond. Just listen. Let them talk. Create a space for a short silence before you go on to the next question.

Active listening is essential. Don't be non-emotive. Make sure the person sees you listening. Give them clues from your body language. Nod your head. React to emotion. Encourage them to "go on" if they stall in the middle of what they are saying.

But listen. Deeply. And make sure you hear what the person is saying.

Listen and Learn Something from Every Meeting

When I started doing Random Days, I had no control over who signed up, no understanding of what we'd discuss, or what I'd get out of the day. I devised a way to start the meeting, which put me in listening mode. I'd start a 15-minute timer (initially an old-school kitchen timer, but eventually my iPhone timer) and say, "It's nice to see you. The next 15 minutes belong to you. I'm happy to discuss anything you'd like. Let's go." And then I'd start the timer.

This ritual put me in a frame of mind to listen. Carefully. Sometimes, there was an awkward silence while the other person collected their thoughts. Other times, they launched into whatever they wanted to discuss. Sometimes, it was a one-way session, and I sat there listening for fifteen minutes. Often, I'd interrupt with a question to clarify something. Occasionally, the person stopped talking, and I asked a question to prompt them to keep talking. And, periodically, they asked me a question, which I responded to but tried to leave open-ended so the other person could answer.

When the timer went off, I politely let the person finish their thought. The timer always helped signal the end, so I never felt impolite, although there were moments when the person would have kept going if I hadn't interrupted them to end the meeting.

I generally didn't take a break, so these days were tiring. I'd do 10 to 15 meetings like this, spending up to four hours on Random Day, where I mostly listened. After one Random Day, I realized I was bored and annoyed. Rather than react in the moment, I let the boredom roll around in the back of my mind, mulling it over, and a few days later, I realized that while I had met a dozen new people, I hadn't learned anything.

So, I added a goal. I decided to learn at least one new thing from every meeting. While focused on listening, I often encountered something I didn't know anything about. At that moment, rather than continue listening passively, I'd interrupt and ask a question. I limited myself to one question to avoid breaking the meeting flow too much or bouncing out of listening mode.

During these meetings, I didn't take notes. But when the timer went off, I tried to move our chat to a follow-up email conversation, by asking them to email me to follow up on a, b, and c. I always finished by telling them to email me about anything anytime.

At the end of Random Day, I sat quietly and considered what I had learned from each meeting. Because I didn't take notes, I viewed this as an exercise to build my listening muscles as I had to remember each conversation and think hard about it. Over time, I could remember better and associate one key thing I learned from each meeting. The bonus of Random Days is that, over time, I became a better listener.

How I Almost Missed Investing in Fitbit

One of the best investments I've ever made was in Fitbit. It was also one of the most exciting, engaging, and challenging companies I've invested in, with extraordinary highs and several near-death experiences. And I almost missed it.

In 2009, I became interested in the quantified self. If you go to my Daytum page,[7] you will see how many miles I ran in which city, how many and what type of books I read, how many airline flights I took

---

7 "BFELD," Daytum, accessed on March 20, 2025, https://www.daytum.com/bfeld. Remember, the Internet never forgets.

on which airlines, and how many times I slept in which town from the beginning of 2009 until I stopped logging this data sometime in 2012.

I started following several people who were blogging about the quantified self. I went to a Meetup and learned about several devices, including the BodyBugg, a Phillips step tracker, a sleep monitor, and a Fitbit. I bought them all and had a bunch of weird devices on my body.

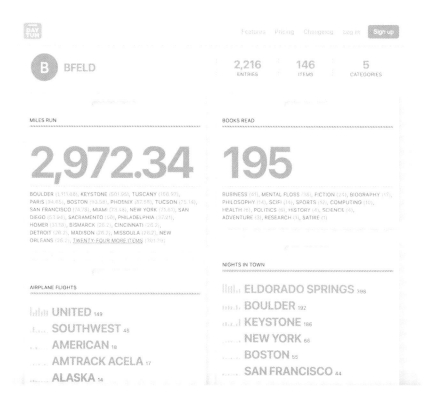

A few months later, I got an email from Jeff Clavier and Jon Callaghan, two VCs with whom I was close friends. I was an LP in Jeff's fund and co-investor in many companies with each of them. The email encouraged me to look at Fitbit, which was raising a round. I expect Jeff and Jon had noticed blog posts about my new personal data obsession. They introduced me to James Park, Fitbit's CEO, and we scheduled a phone call.

A massive snowstorm started on the day of the phone call with James. I was at my house with Amy in Eldorado Springs, and we'd already gotten over a foot of snow, with a prediction of up to four feet. Amy was already preparing to hole up for a few days, and she wanted me to end my work day early to help prepare for being snowed in, something that had happened every few years and that we'd learned to enjoy rather than fight.

"I have one more call, and then I'm done for the day," I hollered from downstairs.

I called James on the phone. All I could think about was finishing the call as quickly as possible.

We did quick intros, and then I asked James to walk me through Fitbit however he wanted. He gave me a brief business overview and started a standard pitch without slides. I was distracted by the snow coming down, now in clumps rather than flakes. James said something about steps, but there was no emotion in what he was saying, and I was distracted by Kenai, our golden retriever, having a crazy-wild-happy-dog-in-the-snow party outside my window.

James mentioned something about health. And possibly a mobile app. USB and ANT connections. More snow.

I told James I needed to finish up because I needed to help my wife get the house ready for the snowstorm we were having. He graciously finished up. I expect he thought I was one of the most useless and distracted VCs he'd ever talked to.

Later that day, the phones went out at our house. The next day, the power went out, but not before I could send James a friendly note saying we were passing. We were stuck in our house for four days before I couldn't bear how I smelled anymore. I hiked out, my brother picked me up, and I showered at his house. We got Amy out a few hours later after someone finally plowed the road in the state park we had to drive on to get to our house.

I had a lot of emails to follow up on, including curious ones from Jon and Jeff. They knew from James that our call didn't go well but were surprised. I told them that while I liked the product, I didn't get excited by James for some reason. They told me I'd read James wrong, that he was an absolute killer—one of their best early-stage CEOs. I said that might be true, but I wanted to spend more time immersed in my quantified self-exploration before choosing an investment.

About nine months later, I received separate notes from Jon and Jeff. Jon was polite and encouraged me to take another look at Fitbit. He described their progress at a high level and told me they hadn't been able to raise a round, so True (Jon's firm), SoftTech (Jeff's firm), and the founders had funded it to get through the year. They were now ready to raise an outside-led round.

Jeff was less polite and more direct. Using his deliciously thick French accent, he said, "Brad, don't be fucking stupid. You need to pay attention to this."[8]

I called each of them. I told them my concern about James. This time, Jon said something that unlocked an insight for me. He said James had a flat, emotionless affect regardless of what was happening.

---

8 Todd Bishop, "How This Reluctant Fitbit Investor Almost Missed a $1.6 Billion Windfall," GeekWire, January 15, 2017, https://www.geekwire.com/2017/reluctant-fitbit-investor-almost-missed-1-6-billion-windfall/.

It didn't matter how exciting, miserable, or complex the situation was. James just dealt with it. You couldn't read him based on his emotion. You had to listen to what he was saying and the words he was using. And you had to watch his facial expressions.

I set up a video conference with James. Amy and I were at our summer place in Homer, Alaska, so I wasn't worried about a snowstorm. I asked James to send me the deck in advance, but I said I wanted to talk and ask him questions rather than go through it. I looked carefully at the deck, came up with a few questions, and had the call.

After 30 minutes, I knew that I wanted to invest in Fitbit. I realized I'd completely missed it the last time by not listening. James behaved exactly how Jon described. My partners and I quickly decided to invest.

The Fitbit investment and experience were incredible for me. I loved working with James and his partner Eric and being on the board with Jon. While our highs and lows were extreme, ringing the bell at the NYSE with the Fitbit team was a peak life moment. And I almost missed it all because the first time I talked to James, I wasn't listening.

The Best Mentor Relationships Eventually Become Two-Way

My best mentors are the ones with whom I have a long-term relationship. They've received as much from me as I've gotten from them. I call this "peer mentoring," and while it can start as an equal relationship, it's wonderful when it evolves from a mentor-mentee relationship.

Use the Other Person's Love Language

Gary Chapman wrote *The Five Love Languages: How to Express Heartfelt Commitment to Your Mate* in 1992. Amy and I read it together in 2015, took the quiz, and talked extensively about it. Understanding each other's love languages transformed our relationship, taking it to a new, more profound level.

The five love languages are:

- words of affirmation
- quality time
- receiving gifts
- acts of service
- physical touch

Everyone has a different primary and secondary love language. The challenge in many relationships is that we don't know our partner's love language and tend to give love how we prefer to receive it rather than how our partner prefers to receive it.[9]

In 2007, Chapman and Paul E. White wrote *The 5 Languages of Appreciation in the Workplace: Empowering Organizations by Encouraging People*, which applied the concept of love language to the workplace. Rather than calling them love languages, they now label them languages of appreciation, modeling them around similar phrases.[10]

While the challenges of applying appreciation in the workplace and love languages in a relationship are different, the basic principle is the same. We tend to show appreciation by how we like to receive it rather than how the other person wants it.

Understanding the other person's language of appreciation can catalyze growth and improvement in communication and relationships. Applying appreciation languages can inspire positive change and foster stronger bonds, whether it's a mentor-mentee relationship or a co-worker dynamic.

Several of My Peer Mentors

I vividly remember the first time I met Len Fassler, sitting in a restaurant in downtown Boston in 1993, wondering, "Who is this guy, and what does he want?" After Len and his partner, Jerry Poch, bought my first company, they took me under their wing and taught me how to acquire other companies. I became part of the acquisition diligence team and traveled with each of them when they met with founders whose companies they were considering buying. They were

9   Gary Chapman. *The Five Love Languages: How to Express Heartfelt Commitment to Your Mate*. Northfield Publishing, 1992.
10 Gary Chapman and Paul White. *The 5 Languages of Appreciation in the Workplace: Empowering Organizations by Encouraging People*. Northfield Publishing, 2007.

incredibly patient with me since I knew nothing about mergers and acquisitions.

When I started making angel investments, Len and Jerry often invested with me and invited me into some of the companies they invested in. After I left AmeriData, my relationship with each of them blossomed differently. Jerry and I made some VC investments together, while Len and I started several companies.

Len and I spent thousands of hours together, and the amount I learned from working with him can't be quantified or categorized. For each of these companies, we were equal partners and co-founders. But Len was the deeply experienced elder, and I was the up-and-comer. I considered him the mentor and myself the mentee.

Later in our relationship, I heard Len often say he learned more from me than he imagined I learned from him. Some of this was his profound humility, but it was also the evolution of our relationship. The dance and intermingling of our experiences, personal philosophies, joys (highs), miseries (lows), and shared time shaped us, even with our 32-year age difference. Over 28 years of working together, we developed a deep, intimate peer relationship.

Len passed away in 2021. I miss him dearly and think about him almost every day. One of my common internal mantras when struggling with something is, "What would Len do?" I'd be honored if someone said I was a vessel for perpetuating and evolving Len's business approach and personal philosophy to people through time and space.

Another peer mentor of mine is my dad's brother, Charlie Feld.

My uncle Charlie has been an extraordinary CIO (chief information officer) for over 50 years and is one of the leaders who created the role in large corporations. He introduced me to my first computer when I was 11 and allowed me to tag along with him for many years. In the early 1980s, as a very young adult, I attended executive meetings at DEC and Lotus which I had no business being in. I learned about EISs (executive information systems) as a teenager and got early access to unreleased computers and software. Charlie taught me how IT and MIS (information technology and management information systems) worked in large companies.

In 1992, Charlie started his company, The Feld Group, when my first company (Feld Technologies) was five years old.

Suddenly, Charlie and I were having peer discussions about our respective consulting businesses. After I sold my company and started investing in companies in 1994, Charlie and I regularly talked about the Internet, which was emerging as something large companies should pay attention to. At the same time, Charlie exposed me to what he was doing to re-architect and modernize enormously complex and disastrous legacy systems at companies like Delta and Burlington Northern. In addition to helping me understand fundamental things about technology at scale, Charlie exposed me to the complexity of these vast organizations.

In 2000, while I was at Mobius Venture Capital, I invested in The Feld Group and joined the board, taking our relationship to a new level. While I was now an investor/partner/board member, our intellectual and emotional intimacy increased. The Feld Group grew until it was acquired in 2004 by EDS. While aspects of my work during this time were excruciating due to the collapse of the Internet bubble, Charlie and The Feld Group gave me a window into the dynamics of enterprise

IT. It was a calming and satisfying counterbalance to the misery of the startups melting down everywhere.

As with my relationship with Len, my relationship with Charlie became a peer-mentor relationship over time. Sure, we had conflicts, disagreements, and disappointments, but each shaped my development on a professional—and personal—level. As mentors, Len and Charlie gave first in every sense of the word.

Be Responsive

A non-responsive mentor baffles me. Being responsive means more than just responding to emails and phone calls. It means more than being on time for meetings, closing the loop on things you commit to doing, and being intellectually and emotionally available to your mentee. These are "hygiene issues"—the price of admission for being a mentor. You won't be effective if you don't do them.

Being responsive means being present and engaging with your mentee, putting yourself in their shoes, and understanding what is happening. Synonyms for the word responsive include receptive, amenable, flexible, sensitive, sympathetic, and aware. These actions require emotional intelligence.

Everyone prioritizes their time differently. You have your unique way of engaging with others. We each get to define our approach to being responsive. Understand this, be clear about it, and then be consistent.

My approach to being responsive has three dimensions: a people hierarchy, interaction dynamics, and baseline expectations.

My people hierarchy is well defined and has been for a long time. In descending order of importance (and responsiveness):

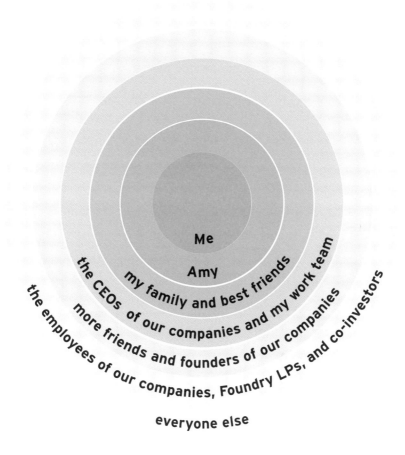

I think of this as concentric circles, with Amy, my family, and my best friends at the center, followed by the people I work most closely with, another set of friends or work colleagues, and then everyone else. I rarely rank individuals ahead of others within one of the circles, but I do plenty of short-term prioritization based on what is happening on any given day.

My interaction dynamics are fuzzier. I don't particularly enjoy talking on the telephone, so I reserve it for people I have a close relationship with. For everyone else, I'd rather interact via email or text message. I used to travel constantly, but since 2020, I have rarely traveled for work. I do scheduled video meetings. When I have an in-person meeting, I enjoy going for a walk. I'm fidgety when I'm in a meeting that lasts longer than an hour, but I've trained myself to be in the moment however long it takes, and if I get impatient, I excuse myself for a little while and regroup. When I'm with someone, I try to shift away from multi-tasking and instead concentrate on one thing at a time, focusing on whatever is happening. When I'm alone in front of my computer, I shift into a "cover a wide range of things" mode, where I do a lot of short tasks, switching between them unless I'm trying to do something that requires deep concentration for an extended period, such as working on a book.

My baseline expectations include responding to every email I get except ones that look like bulk emails or are from a mail merge where "Dear <investor>" is replaced with "Dear Brad." I return all the phone calls I get, although often by email or text message. I try to close the loop on anything someone has asked me to do. When I'm with someone, they have my full attention.

I don't get an A+ on all of this, nor do I view that as necessary. But, by writing it down, I define the structure around what being responsive means.

I'd be a crummy mentor if I did all these things but never listened, wasn't receptive, flexible, or sympathetic. You have to do all of it.

Be Open to Randomness

Many of the great things in my life have occurred due to randomness. While some call this synchronicity or destiny, it results from being open to randomness.

My baseline expectation of responding to every email is an example of being open to randomness. Another is my Random Day concept.

In a busy world with constant performance pressure and expectations around outcomes, having a periodic random day may seem ridiculous. If you think, "That sounds nice and utopian, but I don't have time for that," or "Yeah, Brad, whatever, but you are in a different position in life than I am," I encourage you to reconsider your position.

I am continually amazed by what comes back to me from people I've put energy, time, and resources into without expecting a return. The payoff, financial and non-financial, has been extraordinary.

Responding to Every Email

I regularly get positive feedback about responding to emails. I've responded to all my emails for a long time, ending the day at inbox zero. At some point, I realized that while this was an obsession, it served a purpose. I was responsive to everyone, even the random stuff that came my way, establishing a tone for my engagement.

There were several moments when this was overwhelming. In the early days of the Covid pandemic, I volunteered to be chair of the Colorado Innovation Response Team and head of the Small Business team for the Governor's Economic Stabilization and Growth Council.[11]

---

11 I joked that this sounded like a government committee straight out of *Atlas Shrugged.*

Along with my full-time work at Foundry, I now had a second full-time job. Fortunately, given the Covid crisis, my partners understood and were supportive. I went into a mode I call "the grind" (which some people call "beast mode"), working over 100 hours a week for three months under incredible stress since no one yet understood the pandemic's implications on health, business, society, or anything else. During this period, I tried hard to be emotionally available to the two teams I led and all the companies I was involved with.

This period was as intense as any I'd had in my adult life. The only relief was that I wasn't able to travel and, for several months, I couldn't even leave my house. In the evenings, I'd go downstairs to our TV room to catch up on emails from the day. I'd process what I could during the day, but I'd set up filters for things about Foundry, our companies, my family, and the two volunteer teams that I led. From 7 a.m. to about 7 p.m. each day, I was on back-to-back Zoom meetings (remember that time in your life? Eek!) with one break—lunch with Amy for 30 minutes. If a meeting ended early, I'd spend a few minutes on email. I'd go through more emails during a discussion that I didn't need to pay attention to (and there were many of those, but never for an entire meeting).

When the day ended, my inbox still often had over 500 emails to respond to. Many were from people volunteering, offering suggestions, or complaining about something. Sometimes, they were pertinent questions. Often, they were multiple paragraphs of text from someone I didn't know about something I was trying to figure out in real time.

I sat downstairs with Amy in our TV room and plowed through my email. As soon as I responded, more came in. Some nights, they came in faster than I could clear them. I went in reverse chronological order (from the bottom up), so I just worked my way through them, being as responsive as possible—night after night. I'd always carve out the last hour to go through any replies I'd got, so anything I responded to that generated a reply got another before I went to bed. I caught up on the weekends and tried to stay ahead of the endless waves of emails every week.

I was responsive, using my people hierarchy to prioritize replies when it would have been easy to justify a different modality. I wanted to stay true to my values, and I did.

Adopt at Least One Company Every Single Year

When I advise new mentors, I emphasize the importance of dedicating their efforts to one company during the accelerator program. Rather than spreading their attention thinly across multiple companies, mentors should aim for a more profound engagement with a single company, which can significantly enhance their effectiveness.

In a typical Techstars program with a dozen companies, a mentor who invests an hour a week allocates an hour to each company under their wing. However, by spending a few hours understanding all the companies in the program and then committing an hour per week to just one company, a mentor can delve deep into the company's needs and the founders' vision.

The first few weeks of a Techstars program are called "mentor madness." While founders meet many new people and attend many get-to-know-you types of sessions, there is considerable substance in the mix. Founders experience mentor whiplash, where they get feedback from some mentors that contrasts with feedback from other mentors. Mentor whiplash builds muscle early, as founders learn that feedback from mentors is merely data that they have to process instead of directives to pursue or advice to listen to. Founders quickly realize that feedback from a mentor is one data point, not the answer.

By the end of the first month, companies are encouraged to work with up to five lead mentors for at least an hour a week. Each lead mentor commits to going deep with the company. The most effective lead mentors limit themselves to one or two companies during the program.

Great mentors do this year after year, program after program. You don't magically become a great mentor overnight. I've seen many experienced founders, investors, and service providers show up as mentors for the first time and be ineffective.

While mentors benefit from experience and feedback, nothing helps them improve more than practice by trying new things, seeing what works, observing the results, and helping others. Listen to the founders' feedback on what is helping them and what is getting in their way, slowing them down, confusing them, or undermining them.

A mentor has a limited capacity to mentor. Go deep with one company at a time, and do it repeatedly.

Emotional Intelligence

Mentors quickly develop functional experience. For many, it's innate based on their historical work and leadership experiences, especially if they were founders or CEOs.

Mastering emotional intelligence (EQ, or "emotional quotient") is much more challenging. The concept is relatively new in business. It was coined in 1990 by John D. Mayer of UNH and Peter Salovey of Yale in an article titled "Emotional Intelligence"[12] and popularized by Dan Goleman in his 1995 book *Emotional Intelligence: Why It Can Matter More Than IQ.*

---

12 Peter Salovey and John D. Mayer, "Emotional Intelligence," *Imagination, Cognition and Personality,* 9 (3), March 1990: 185–211. https://journals.sagepub.com/doi/10.2190/DUGG-P24E-52WK-6CDG.

EQ is complicated because it requires a person to be self-aware, understand their emotions and how these affect their behavior, and manage these emotions to interact effectively with others. It also requires understanding other people's feelings and how to respond to them productively and appropriately. Finally, EQ requires understanding how to communicate with others effectively and read nonverbal cues.

Being a mentor is not just about guiding others; it's also a fantastic opportunity for personal growth. It's a chance to develop and hone your EQ skills, understand and manage your emotions, and interact effectively with others. The problems you are exploring and addressing are your mentees', not yours. You don't need to solve them. You don't need to feel stressed by them. You don't need to get into conflict around solving them. Instead, you can observe and listen to your mentee, provide empathy, and ask guiding questions. This process can be incredibly fulfilling and lead to a deeper understanding of yourself.

In the context of mentoring, EQ is paramount. Your body language and facial expressions matter. How you engage with your mentee, especially if you see them struggling with their emotions, is critical. You can better understand their emotional state and respond appropriately by paying attention to their nonverbal cues. Using their language of appreciation to give them positive reinforcement, especially as they have breakthroughs, reinforces your support. Since you have to learn their emotional context to be effective, working with fewer companies allows you to get better by going deeper with the one you are working with.

Betting on Gearbox

We ran the fourth Techstars Boulder program in 2010. It took place in The Bunker, a dingy office in the basement of a building in downtown Boulder. The Bunker used to be a health club, so it still had hot tubs in the bathrooms and corkboards on the walls. It was a great startup space.

I remember sitting with David Cohen and Nicole Glaros, going through the 40 finalists. We had a simple selection process at the time. David and Nicole did the first pass of all the applications, ran some events, and met with some of the founders. They narrowed the scope to under 40 companies, including their top five picks. Then, we tried to figure out which ones we wanted, in ranked order from #6 to #20. After this, they tried to recruit the top 10, and if people passed for any reason, they went to #11, then #12, and so on until they filled up 10 slots.

We were going through the list, and a company called Gearbox came up.

David immediately said, "I don't know what to do with these two guys. They have an idea for a hardware company. It doesn't feel like it fits in Techstars. And I think their idea is stupid."

He was being nice—David is always nice—but he was saying, "I hate this one."

Nicole said, "I love Adam and Ian (the founders). They are awesome and crazy smart. Yeah, their idea isn't great, but so what? Working with them could be amazing and so much fun."

I listened to them volley things back and forth a little before responding.

"Let's just fucking try it. The worst case is that it fails, and we learn that a hardware company doesn't work well in an accelerator. I'll be one of their lead mentors. Let's try this and learn from it."

We decided to invite them to the program, and they accepted. At the end of the first week, after they had met with several mentors, I had my first meeting with them.

While Ian looked on, Adam shyly said, "We are having trouble figuring out what to do."

I said, "What do you mean?"

"We've been working on several ideas all week, and some mentors like one of them, some like another, and no one likes the third."

"What are the ideas?"

Looking extremely bored, Adam started walking me through the idea with which they had applied to the program: using an iPhone to turn lights on and off or open a garage door. Remember, this was 2010, so it was a new idea.

"Tell me the next idea."

Adam was more animated this time, like someone who has woken up from a nap and asked a question while they were rubbing the sleep out of their eyes.

"Tell me the last idea."

Adam jumped up and stood on top of the table.

"It's a ball that is a robot controlled by a smartphone. You can play games with it, roll it around, and torture your cat."

"Um, you seem excited about the robotic ball. Why the confusion about what to do?"

"We can't develop a business model for it, and none of the other mentors like it better than the other two ideas."

I sat there for about 15 seconds to see if Ian had anything to say. He didn't. But he was smiling a little.

"Guys, of the three ideas, the only one that lights you up is the robot ball. At this stage, no one knows the answer, only questions. The default business model is to sell a robot ball to people. I have no idea if that will work, but it'd be a blast to try."

We talked about robotic balls, how hard they were to create technically, all the engineering challenges associated with them, and why they didn't exist. Maybe they didn't exist not because no one cared, but because they were complicated to create.

Gearbox became Sphero, and Foundry led the seed investment. In 2015, *Star Wars: The Force Awakens* came out, and BB-8, which Sphero built, was everywhere. Today, Sphero is a leader in programmable robots, EdTech, computer science, and STEM education tools for students and educators in PK-12. The original round robotic ball (now known as Sphero BOLT and Mini) is a vital part of the product line and is an extremely popular learning robot in schools worldwide.

Clearly Separate Opinion from Fact

We live in a world of assertions. Many of us have a fuzzy line between opinions and facts. We interpret facts to fit our views and broaden our opinions beyond the underlying data. Opinions are often formed from a single idea rather than a set of facts, lacking a broad context and perspective.

Founders, investors, and mentors often assert an opinion as fact. I know I fall into this trap regularly and frequently catch others doing it too. When I challenge someone based on my data, they often revert to a position where they express an opinion. If I hadn't challenged them, everyone else hearing the statement might view it as a fact.

Opinions are useful. But they are different from facts. Knowing what you are saying and framing it as an opinion, fact, or hypothesis is crucial for effective communication.

In addition to separating opinions from facts, it is helpful to separate data from facts. While data is factual, the conclusion from the data is often an opinion or a hypothesis. If you assert the data as a fact and start to extrapolate from this fact or encourage a mentee to do something based on it, you can quickly go down a blind alley.[13]

---

13 If you are intrigued by this, I encourage you to read Daniel Kahneman's brilliant book, *Thinking, Fast and Slow*.

People always get trapped in the fact/opinion/data matrix. As a mentor, be careful and precise about what you say. Your goal is to help your mentee, not be the most intelligent person in the room.

The Importance of Stating Your Hypothesis

A startup is not a one-time event but an ongoing series of experiments. You propose a hypothesis, run an experiment, and learn from the results. If the experiment doesn't yield the expected outcome, it's not a failure but a learning opportunity. Revise your hypothesis, conduct a new experiment, and continue this iterative process. If the experiment succeeds, you can validate your hypothesis and proceed with more of what worked.

While mentors can provide facts or data, their most valuable role is helping the mentee form a hypothesis. A mentor may not always have the answer to a particular question, but they can guide the mentee in developing a better hypothesis. Furthermore, the mentor can assist in setting up an experiment to test the theory, interpreting the results, forming a conclusion, and, if necessary, stating a new hypothesis.

However, many mentees are just looking for the answer. So, unless the mentor clearly states that what they say is a hypothesis, a mentee may accept it as fact.

The Parable of a House Cat, Zebra Finch, Owl, and Mountain Lion

Let's try an entrepreneurial koan to change the pace.

Imagine four different animals in a conversation, each with a personality.

The House Cat has strong opinions that are loosely held but can't express a hypothesis.

The Owl asks questions of everyone.

The Mountain Lion pays careful attention to body language.

The Zebra Finch listens to everyone before stating their opinion.

The House Cat, Zebra Finch, Owl, and Mountain Lion walk into a bar.

"Give me a gin and tonic," says the House Cat to the bartender.

"Why do you want one of those?" asks the Owl.

"Okay, I'll take a rum and Coke."

The Owl asks, "Why did you change your mind?"

The House Cat jumps up on the bar and says, "I just feel like it."

The Owl flutters up to the bar next to the House Cat, which is looking at the Mountain Lion staring at them, but quickly breaks eye contact.

"Would something different be better?" asks the Owl.

"Yes. I want a Hibiki 21," says the House Cat.

As the bartender turns to get a Hibiki down from the wall, the Mountain Lion leaps over and eats the House Cat in one gulp.

"That's what you get for constantly changing your mind when someone asks you too many questions," said the Zebra Finch.

Pro-tip: Don't break eye contact with the Mountain Lion when the Mountain Lion is staring at you.

Hold Information in Confidence

For many years, I've refused to sign NDAs as they are lightweight fiction, especially in early-stage companies. Instead, I operate on a FriendDA[14] basis. It's not official or legally binding, but implies that you will hold information in confidence if a founder bares their soul.

This behavior can be tricky. It's hard to know what is confidential, a secret, something someone is merely pondering, a brilliant new idea, something that conflicts with something you know about, or something that will upset someone if it gets around.

There's a simple approach to this: use your judgment. If you are uncertain, ask the person who gave you the information if it is confidential.

We operate this way at Foundry. We don't sign NDAs.[15] If you don't trust us, don't share something with us. If you don't want us to know something, that's fine. If we must hold something in confidence, feel free to say so. Assume we are respectful and conscientious about what we can and can't share.

Fundamentally, this is an issue of reputation. It's impossible to have an effective mentor-mentee relationship without trust. A legal document doesn't create trust or meaningful recourse if trust is violated. When someone I know develops a reputation as an information leaker by inappropriately trading in information or violating confidence,

---

14 See https://friendda.org/ for a clever description.
15 I first wrote about this in 2006: "Why Most VC's Don't Sign NDAs," Brad Feld, February 14, 2006, https://feld.com/archives/2006/02/why-most-vcs-dont-sign-ndas/.

I don't stop interacting with them. However, I'm more circumspect and cautious about what I discuss with them.

When someone violates my trust, especially regarding confidential information, I am responsible for addressing the situation. I am specific about what and how the confidential information was exposed and what my expectations were. Then, I give the person a second chance.

Building Trust

In 2014, Reid Hoffman and Ben Casnocha wrote an influential book titled *The Alliance: Managing Talent in the Networked Age.*[16] Their premise was that the modern employer-employee relationship was broken. On Day 1, your manager welcomes you to the family and expresses their hope you'll be with the company for a long time. You express your excitement, appreciation, and loyalty to your new employer. You then get handed off to HR, who tells you that you are on a 90-day probation and an "at will" employee whom the company can fire for any reason.

Oops. You go home at the end of the first day with broken trust. Reid and Ben developed a new concept called "the alliance." Instead of thinking of employees as a family or free agents, think of them as allies on a tour of duty. Employment should be an alliance, a mutually beneficial deal with explicit terms between independent players. Or, like Netflix, consider yourself a team, not a family.[17]

Elements of the alliance apply to mentorship, especially around trust. As a mentor, you receive all kinds of information from the mentee, including ideas, unique intellectual property, or deeply

16 Reid Hoffman, Ben Casnocha, and Chris Yeh. *The Alliance: Managing Talent in the Networked Age.* Harvard Business Review Press, 2014.
17 Marc Randolph, "You Are a Team, Not a Family," Medium, September 20, 2023, https://mbrandolph.medium.com/you-are-a-team-not-a-family-7d4b626c4de8.

personal emotions. As a mentor, you must confidentially hold all this information while steadily and continuously building credibility with your mentee. One wrong move immediately destroys trust.

When a Mentor Patents What a Mentee Is Doing

While an explosive breach of trust between a mentor and mentee does not often occur at Techstars, it does happen.

I was catching up on email one day when I got a phone call from the CEO of a company.

"You are not going to believe this," he said.

"Good or bad?" I asked.

"Bad, and crazy, and absurd."

"Okay. Go ahead." I put on my Something New Is Fucked Up in My World Every Day mindset.[18]

"Joe[19] patented our product." Joe was a mentor for Techstars and the company, which had gone through Techstars several years earlier.

"Huh, what?"

"Yeah. Our patent is still under review, but Joe's patent was just issued. And it's our product. It's our IP. We described it during Techstars when he met with us regularly."

"Let me call Joe and see what he's trying to accomplish."

I called Joe. He explained that he'd come up with the idea several years earlier. He said it took some time when I asked him why his patent filing was six months after the company went through the Techstars program. I asked him if he'd built the product. He said no. I asked him if he knew he was violating mentor norms and stepping on

---

18 "Something New Is Fucked Up in My World Every Day," Brad Feld, April 1, 2015, https://feld.com/archives/2015/04/something-new-fucked-world-every-day/.
19 Not his real name.

the IP of a company he had mentored. He denied this. I asked him how he justified things.

"I came up with the idea."

"Are you certain you had the idea before you were a mentor to this company?"

There was a pause. Then, "I think so. Yes."

"Are you sure? Can you explain the software algorithms required to make this product work?"

"That's not what the patent is about."

Our conversation continued for a few more minutes. I called the CEO back, told him what had happened, and suggested he talk to IP counsel about invalidating Joe's patent due to prior art. It took a year and some money, but the company did invalidate Joe's patent. Eventually, the company's patent was issued.

We will all remember this forever, and not in a good way.

Clearly Commit to Mentor or Do Not. Either Is Fine.

At a moment of despair, Yoda said to Luke, "Do. Or do not. There is no try." The phrase has been one of my favorites when applied to anything. However, many people misinterpret this scene from *The Empire Strikes Back*. Let's deconstruct it.

Luke and Yoda are on Dagobah, where Luke traveled at the behest of Obi-Wan Kenobi to get training from Yoda, who lives there. Since every good *Star Wars* scene needs something for the hero to overcome, Luke crashes his X-Wing in a bog and is stranded on the planet until he figures out how to get it free.

This moment is a perfect setup for some Yoda training, which begins with floating rocks and gymnastics, but Luke eventually loses his balance and collapses. The commotion causes the X-Wing to sink entirely into the swamp.

Luke says, "Oh, no. We'll never get it out now."

Yoda angrily stamps his foot and says, "So certain are you. Always with you it cannot be done. Hear you nothing that I say?"

"Master, moving stones around is one thing. This is totally different."

"No! No different! Only different in your mind. You must *unlearn* what you have learned."

"All right, I'll give it a try."

The famous moment then occurs when Yoda exclaims, "No! Try not. Do. Or do not. There is no try."

But the excellent stuff comes moments after Luke tries again and fails. After Luke expresses his discouragement, Yoda lectures him about the Force. Luke tells Yoda he wants the impossible, and Yoda responds by levitating the X-Wing out of the swamp and gently putting it down on the beach.

In awe, Luke says, "I don't . . . I don't believe it."

Yoda replies, "That is why you fail."

The classical interpretation follows the literal interpretation: Either do something. Or don't do something. But don't merely try to do something. Unfortunately, "do" is often linked to success, and "don't do" is related to failure.

Creating a company is an endless series of experiments. When the experiment fails, develop a new hypothesis and run another experiment. When the experiment succeeds, do more of it.

Consequently, there is a lot of failure in creating a company. And, no matter how successful a person is, their life has many failed experiences woven throughout.

Yoda is not talking about success or failure. He is talking about "belief" and, specifically, belief in oneself. If you don't believe in yourself, you will fail. While you won't succeed by merely believing in yourself, belief is table stakes for succeeding.

Belief and commitment are close cousins. Rewriting Yoda's mantra, we get, "Commit. Or do not commit. There is no try."

If you are going to mentor someone, commit to it. Your mentee is relying on you. Don't drop balls. Don't miss meetings. Be responsive.

And if you can't fulfill your commitment, say so. Don't ever leave your mentee hanging.

Give, Don't Ask

The following is an email from a close friend who asked how I reconcile a particular issue related to Give First.

> I was thinking of you yesterday. I recently met with someone in town who was looking to connect. I took the meeting because, well, I always take such meetings. I'm wired that way; you never know what good things can come from such random meetings. So I love doing them. But yesterday, the person I met with showed up with an agenda and, at the top of his list, was "Give First to <my organization> and <me>." He had an agenda. He had an ask of me, but he wanted to "give first" by asking how he could help me. Moreover, he immediately put me in debt to him by saying, "Before we begin, let me ask, How can I help you?" While I don't have many asks, it still felt yucky, insincere, and manipulative.

Asking someone how you can help them at the beginning of a meeting is a misunderstanding of Give First. While well-intentioned, it shifts the burden of responsibility.

Consider taking the opposite approach. Do your research before you meet. Understand the person's or organization's goals. Often, you can figure out a short-term need with a few minutes of research. Then, when you meet, prepare for the conversation and listen to where it goes. In real time, offer to do something that fits with what you are hearing or what you expect the goals or short-term needs to be.

This preparation shouldn't have to be an explicit part of the conversation (e.g., "I'm going to Give First to you by doing the following"). Instead, it should be completely non-transactional—you are not doing something to earn anything, including brownie points. Instead, you are operating in a Give First framework, where you are willing to put energy into something without expecting anything in return. Ideally, you'll do something helpful for the other party. Not once, but as part of establishing and developing a deeper relationship from a non-transactional perspective.

It's easy to fall into the trap of mechanizing the Give First philosophy. It's explicitly called Give First, and not Tell Me What I Can Do to Help You, to stimulate you—the giver—to do the work of figuring out what is helpful.

A Diversion about Just Doing Things

While this story has nothing to do with entrepreneurship, it has everything to do with Give First.

How often has someone asked, "What can I get you?" Or "What kind of gift would {your significant other} like?" Or "What can I do to be helpful?"—especially when someone is distressed.

Here's an example: The wife of one of my best friends had routine surgery. At about noon, he texted, "The surgery seems to have gone fine. I'm just waiting for them to finish up." Then, nothing for several hours. I texted, Slacked, and emailed him. Nothing. Then, a brief message: "There have been complications. She's still in surgery." Then nothing.

The surgery was happening in Denver. It was now the end of the day and Amy and I were getting ready to go out to dinner. We were worried about our friends, and I suddenly blurted out, "What are we doing? We should go check on our friends." We canceled our dinner plans, got in our car, and drove to the hospital. We figured out where our friends were in the hospital. When we walked into the room and my friend saw us, he broke down in tears.

His wife had just come out of a surgery that ended up taking eight hours and had life-threatening complications. We just sat with our friend and his mother-in-law. Eventually, he was able to see his wife for thirty minutes. After he came out, he looked utterly exhausted. Amy put her arm around him and said, "Okay. Time to feed you." Our friend's mother-in-law had said they hadn't eaten all day. Our friend didn't say anything but just followed us. About 15 minutes later, he dug into what he described as "the most amazing chicken parmesan I've ever eaten." We were at a chain called Carrabba's Italian Grill, so it probably wasn't the food, but you get the idea.

His wife was in great distress and danger for the first 24 hours. Ultimately, she recovered completely. When you know someone is in distress, don't ask. Just do. Maybe this is something Grogu will eventually say.

Know What You Don't Know. Say "I Don't Know" When You Don't Know

We all know the Smartest Guys in the Room. I find them insufferable, and I've nicknamed them Smartypants. Unfortunately, Smartypants exist in my world because they inhabit the bodies and souls of some founders and investors. Regardless of how they manifest themselves, Smartypants are tiresome, and when there are two of them in the room, watch out.

The best mentors are not Smartypants. While great mentors know a lot and have had plenty of experiences, they always learn. The best mentor-mentee relationships are peer relationships, where the mentor learns as much from the mentee as they teach. There's no room in this relationship for Smartypants.

I know a lot about some things. And I know very little or nothing about a lot of things. My business and technology experience is deep in software, where I consider the hardware companies I invest in as "software wrapped in plastic." At the essence of it, I know software the best.

But I don't know everything about software. And I especially don't know vertical markets. I've consciously stayed horizontal in my investing. Ask me about a vertical market, whether it be entertainment, real estate, insurance, auto, food, energy, or financial services, and I'll approach it with a beginner's mind.

Often, something generic will apply to a vertical market. But when asked about something structural, even though I've had many different experiences, read a zillion articles over the years, and might have some opinions, as a mentor, I'm quick to say, "I don't know," unless I'm confident that I do.

When I find myself in an "I don't know" situation as a mentor, I figure out who I can refer the founder to who might know something relevant. And just because I don't know doesn't mean I'm not curious about discovering more. I'll stay engaged and hear what the founder, or the person I refer the founder to, has to say so that I learn from the experience.

I say "I don't know," or some version of it, multiple times a day.

I Don't Know How to Help You

At the end of a conversation, someone periodically asks me, "Is there something I can do for you?" I'll answer, "Do something helpful to something or someone in my world." I occasionally get a response like, "I'm not sure what to do to help you." Over time, I modified my response to, "Do whatever you think is useful to grow your startup community."

I thought this was a good answer until someone paused, looked at me directly, and said, "I've heard you talk about Give First. I think I understand, but I don't know how to help you."

Give First doesn't have to be reciprocal. If it were, I'd have called it Give-to-Get. It's spontaneously being able to help someone because you can, not because you feel indebted to them and feel the need to repay them for their help. While it's okay to ask what you can do for someone as an expression of gratitude, it's much better to do something for them in the future.

Today, when someone asks how they can help me after I've helped them, I say, "You don't need to do anything for me."

Be a Connector When You Don't Know

I've never invested directly in cleantech or climate-related companies. However, I'm enthusiastic about the innovation in these categories, so I helped create the Techstars Sustainability Accelerator in partnership with The Nature Conservancy. I'm also an investor in several funds, such as USV Climate, Lowercarbon, and Moxxie, which invest heavily in this sector.

I could invest substantial time and energy[20] in learning about technology and innovation related to climate and cleantech, but I've chosen not to. Instead, I try to be a connector.

It would be easy to masquerade as someone who has a clue. I could easily trade on my reputation in entrepreneurship. I could pretend to evaluate companies, asking thoughtful and challenging questions, even if I didn't know how to assess the substance of the answers or what the answers meant. But that's the opposite of being useful.

As a connector, I could pretend to know the value of the information I shared and the people I connected with the founders. However, given my lack of domain knowledge, this would be disingenuous.

As with almost all introductions I make, I use a double opt-in approach. First, I ask the person if I can introduce them to X, Y, and Z. Assuming they say yes, I ask them for a forwardable email. I then forward this email to X, Y, and Z, telling them I didn't know anything

---

20 See what I did there?

about the specific project but thought the person was credible enough to see if they wanted an intro. If they do, I ask them to tell me. Otherwise, I tell them to delete the email. I make the intro if any of X, Y, or Z respond.

While this often doesn't generate interest, it's more helpful than ignoring the person in a situation where you don't know anything about what they are doing.

Guide, Don't Control

Throughout Techstars, we tell the founders, "It's your company." The founders decide what to do; everything they hear from mentors is just data.

Many mentors are successful CEOs who are used to being in control. However, they don't control anything in the context of being a mentor. The most they can do is be a guide.

The best investors understand this. One of my favorite sayings as an investor is, "I only want to make one decision about a company—whether or not I support the CEO. If I support the CEO, I work for her. If I don't support the CEO, I need to do something about this, which doesn't mean firing her, but rather trying to get back to where I support her."

As a mentor, you have only one decision: whether or not to continue mentoring. If you do, your job is to support and guide the founders.

Consider the following situation. The company has three founders. While one of them is the CEO, it's unclear whether it's the right one. In addition, two of the founders are struggling with the third founder.

It would be easy to assess the situation and tell the founders what to do, but that's not your job. Instead, help them understand the problem. Invest time with each founder, listening and keeping an open mind. Then, surface the issues, helping them realize what's happening.

Discuss the situation with the founders and guide them to a resolution, but don't tell them what to do.

Be a guide, not the problem solver or the decider. At some point, it is appropriate to say what you would do if you found yourself in a similar situation. But don't force this outcome, nor be judgmental if the founders go down a different path.

Collaborative Negotiation

As a mentor, you will often find yourself involved in giving a founder feedback about a negotiation between founders, a founder and a prospective employee, a founder and an investor, or a founder and another company. Remember your role as a guide. It's not your responsibility to solve the problem but to collaborate with the founder to help get to a successful outcome.

There are many different ways to negotiate, but one approach is to be unpredictable: Load up your asks on the front end so you can easily give on some of them. Be emotionally random, throwing a fit and becoming frustrated, even if you aren't, to put the other person on edge. Respond quickly to some things, then go silent for a day and see if the other person gets rattled and reaches out. Hide behind others, saying you must check on something with your colleagues.

I find this strategy tiresome and prefer a collaborative approach to negotiations. While some aspects of negotiation are win-lose, many are win-win, an idea that Roger Fisher and William Ury developed in 1984 in their classic book *Getting to Yes: Negotiating an Agreement Without Giving In*. While win-win may not apply to a hostage situation, many negotiations can have this outcome.

As a mentor, founders view you as an honest intermediary. You can see all sides of an issue and try to help the counterparties reach a solution, especially over a long period when you end up in negotiations with the same party on the other side. Remember, help guide the parties to an outcome.

Finally, here's a bonus hint for negotiating with someone who is not collaborative. Whenever the other party says, "This is my best and final offer," test the statement. Ask for a few more things. Or, just go silent for a few days and see what happens. Try to determine if it is, in fact, their best and final offer. It rarely is.

Just Tell Me the Answer

I'm in the CEO-only session of a FullContact board meeting. Bart Lorang, the CEO, is struggling with a challenging issue. The other board members are entirely in Socratic mode, asking endless questions. Bart tries to answer them but gets frustrated, especially when he doesn't have good answers.

I tell a story from another company because I think it's relevant and will indirectly help Bart answer the questions better. However, my story doesn't land well, and everyone looks perplexed. A few more questions follow, including one that incorporates my story but not how I had hoped.

I tell another story that addresses the issue more precisely and in more detail. Bart gets agitated and walks around the room. Another board member asks me a question about the story that has nothing to do with the issue Bart is wrestling with. I start to answer the question, but I realize I'm rambling far off topic, so I look at Bart.

Bart looks straight at me and says, "Brad, would you just tell me the fucking answer."

I tell him the answer.

Sometimes, you must suspend your role as a guide, especially if the founder asks you to.

Accept and Communicate with Other Mentors That Get Involved

In an early Techstars program, two mentors were well known to me. Each was a co-founder of a different but competitive company and was technical, brilliant, and capable. Not surprisingly, they gravitated toward mentoring the same Techstars company.[21]

One co-founder lived in Boulder, and the other lived in Denver. They were bitter rivals. While each company was successful, their paths ended up being different, with one going public and the other being acquired.

These co-founders had never interacted directly, but the CEOs of each company had, and they had had some rough interactions. I was friends with both CEOs, but after a failed mediation session, I gave up and let them be at war.

As a result, each of these mentors thought the other was an evil person. When they ended up in the same room with the same Techstars company as part of a mentor session, an awkward moment ensued. Fortunately, I was in the room, so I encouraged them to let their pasts be history and to move on. I anticipated they'd like each other if they had an opportunity to reset things and work together on something.

In a meeting a few weeks later, they gave the founder wildly different feedback on the company's direction. Everyone in the meeting was aware of their past and there was a lot of tension in the room. Their

---

21 This story is a combination of several situations rather than a singular event.

disagreement turned into a debate, and the two mentors went deeper into their thoughts, hashing out their different perspectives, which evolved into a fascinating and fun discussion. Along with the Techstars founder, everyone else in the room just sat silently and observed. Ultimately, one of the mentors changed their perspective based on the debate and they converged on the feedback they gave the founder.

Soon after this meeting, the two co-founders discussed their past feelings toward each other. Since they had never met, they realized their negative feelings resulted from the hostile relationship between their CEOs. They turned out to enjoy working together and subsequently became good friends.

The founder they were mentoring benefited significantly from their involvement. Given their different experiences in similar, competitive businesses, the mentors were instrumental in the company's early development. While they didn't agree on everything, they complemented each other nicely. Consequently, the founder benefited from both mentors instead of having to make a Sophie's Choice by selecting one of them.

Sharing Time

Quality time is Amy's love language.[22] It took me a while to figure this out. For the first 20-something years of our relationship, I constantly traveled for work, so we were apart much more than we were together. While we eventually figured out how to make our relationship thrive, I continually undermined my behavior by not communicating consistently in Amy's love language.

---

22 Chapman, *The Five Love Languages*.

Covid changed that. For almost three years, we spent every day together. We both stopped traveling, at first because of the Covid lockdowns, but then because of our fear of getting Covid. I have a respiratory issue and take COPD medication. I also have an anxiety disorder (OCD) and am a germaphobe. Oh, and science.

By year three, we decided we liked this way of living much better.

As it turns out, quality time is also my love language. Ideally, for both of us, it's quality time with a small number of people rather than a big group. I enjoy four people or fewer and tolerate anything up to about 10 people. However, I actively dislike groups of more than 10 people. While I can function in large groups, they exhaust me. In contrast, being with one to three other people energizes me, and I particularly treasure one-on-one time.

One day, while we were having morning coffee, Amy commented on "sharing time" instead of "spending time together." When we have morning coffee, we share time, actively talking and engaging. When we are both lying on the couch reading a book, we are spending time together. Both are good, but morning coffee is better.

Morning coffee is quality time but with bonus points of engaging with each other. During morning coffee, we exchange information, look at each other, and connect emotionally. I notice this happening at night when we take a break from reading and talk about something for a little while. It's more powerful than just being together.

I don't want to spend time with people; I want to share time with them. When I mentor, I'm wholly present. I share time. That's why I don't enjoy coffee meetings or work meals. Yeah, we talk, but we also eat. And when there are more than four people at the table, I can't concentrate on sharing time because there are too many distractions. I want to be fully engaged.

Really Spending Time Together

Once a year, Ben Casnocha shares time with me and Amy. Maybe it's in Boulder. Or Aspen. Or Homer. Or Rancho Valencia. He sets aside a few days, often over a long weekend, and comes to wherever we happen to be.

I met Ben when he was 14. His father knew one of my Mobius partners and finagled a pitch meeting with us. I fondly remember sitting in one of our meeting rooms with a tall, gangly teenager wearing a white shirt and a yellow power tie pitching his company, Comcate.

We didn't invest in Comcate, but I started spending time with Ben. When I was in the Bay Area, we'd get together for lunch or dinner a few times a year. Amy tagged along once, and a wonderful personal friendship began between them. We have ended up loving Ben like an aunt and uncle love a cherished nephew.

After a year of college, Ben came and visited us in Homer. I could tell he was anxious when he got off the plane. After dropping off his stuff at our house, we went to Fat Olives for pizza.

Ben quickly brought up college.

"I'm not enjoying college. I think it's a waste of time."

"Tell me more," I said.

Amy and I stopped eating and gave Ben our undivided attention. He described his experience and aspirations and explained what he felt he was missing. We asked a few questions to prompt him to keep talking, and then we asked what he wanted to do instead. He was remarkably clear about how he wanted to spend his time and why it was impossible to do this in college.

"Are you asking for permission to stop going to college?" I asked.

Ben paused for a moment.

"Sort of. I know it's not a popular idea. Most people are telling me to gut it out. Or get over myself and embrace college."

Amy said, "Ben, you are remarkable. A lot of people need college for various reasons. I needed it to escape everything that could have held me back. I needed the credentials. I needed the confidence boost. I needed to get away from Alaska. You don't need any of these things. You don't need college."

I said, "I agree."

Ben smiled for the first time since he had stepped off the plane.

Amy was right. Ben is remarkable.[23] And he didn't need college.

---

23 See https://casnocha.com/about for more on Ben. If you are wondering, he is in the "my family and best friends" section of my hierarchy.

Be Optimistic

As a mentor, your job is not to solve a founder's problem. Instead, you help, listen, and provide data and feedback based on your experience. While this can be done from different perspectives, it is most helpful from an optimistic frame of reference.

Imagine you are mentoring a CEO who is struggling with a co-founder who has become unpredictable, inconsistent, and subdued.

Now, assume you also had a problematic co-founder experience in your last company. While the dynamics were different, the experience ended poorly, with your co-founder leaving the company. While you and your co-founder haven't spoken since you split up, your business succeeded and was acquired for a life-changing amount of money for each of you. Your situation didn't result in a sustained relationship with your co-founder, but it was financially rewarding for both of you. You still carry this conflict in your head and your body.[24]

On the one hand, you are pessimistic about where things between the CEO you are mentoring and their co-founder will end up. Conversely, you know the company can succeed even if their relationship fails.

You learned a lot from your experience with your co-founder. Each of you made mistakes. This behavior hurt both of you and negatively impacted the company. Your struggle was public, ruining relationships with others who felt they needed to choose sides.

---

24 Bessel van der Kolk. *The Body Keeps the Score: Brain, Mind, and Body in the Healing of Trauma.* Penguin Publishing Group, 2014.

It is difficult to be optimistic in this context. However, start from a positive frame of reference. Talk openly with the CEO about what you and your co-founder did wrong as you tried to address your conflict. Be clear about how things could have turned out differently. Be introspective and speak from experience instead of giving advice. Remember to reinforce that your business was successful even though your relationship with your co-founder failed.

Let the CEO have their own experience as they resolve things with their co-founder. Try to positively influence the situation and encourage them to do the work involved, even if they end up parting ways.

Facing Reality

When trying to be optimistic about a problematic situation, it's easy to tip into denial. This dynamic is particularly dangerous for a mentor, and you should be realistic with your mentee.

There's no value in helping someone feel better in the short term while at the same time denying reality. Whatever is going on will eventually come to the surface, and you and your mentee will ultimately have to deal with it.

However, you can face reality while being optimistic.

There is a beautiful fable about the Buddhist saint Milarepa,[25] who left his cave to gather firewood. When he returned, demons had taken over his cave—there were demons everywhere!

When he saw them, his first thought was, "I have got to get rid of them!" He lunged toward them, chased them, and tried to force them out of his cave. The demons were unfazed. The more he chased them,

---

25 I first heard this fable from Jerry Colonna in 2015 and wrote about it: Feld, "Something New Is Fucked Up in My World Every Day."

the more comfortable and settled they became. Realizing that his efforts to run them out had failed miserably, Milarepa decided to try a new approach and teach them the dharma.

So he took his seat and began. After a while, he looks around and realizes all the demons are still there. At this point, Milarepa lets out a deep breath of surrender, knowing now that these demons will not be manipulated into leaving and that maybe he has something to learn from them. He looks deeply into the eyes of each demon and bows, saying, "It looks like we're going to be here together. I open myself to whatever you have to teach me."

Immediately, all the demons but one disappear. The one left is incredibly fierce, with flaring nostrils and dripping fangs. So Milarepa lets go even further. Stepping over to it, he offers himself completely, holding nothing back. "Eat me if you wish." He places his head in the demon's mouth, and at that moment, the giant demon bows low and dissolves into space.

Don't be in denial when in challenging situations. But stay optimistic while putting your head in the demon's mouth.

Staying Optimistic When Firing Someone

I've fired many CEOs. I've also fired partners from each VC firm I've co-founded, and when I was a CEO, I fired employees. It's never fun.

I remember when my partner, Ryan McIntyre, fired a CEO for the first time. He was incredibly nervous. Just before the meeting, he met another VC on the company board. This VC wasn't new to firing CEOs and jokingly told Ryan that he saved firing CEOs for his birthday. They went to the meeting together and did their best.

The first time I fired an employee was torturous for me. It took me and my partner, Dave, several months to decide to fire this employee.

While agonizing about the situation, I spent a weekend at the inaugural Birthing of Giants event at MIT Endicott House. My roommate, Alan Treffler, had to listen to me endlessly quiz him on how to fire someone. I talked to at least a dozen other participants, all of whom were theoretically peers, but as one of the youngest participants with one of the smallest companies, they all felt like mentors to me. In every case, they encouraged me to fire this employee quickly and with a positive attitude. I regularly heard, "The person you will fire is probably unhappy. They know things aren't working well. Firing them will be better for them as well as your company. They may not realize it when you fire them, but if you do it gracefully, they might eventually realize this."

Even after deciding to do it, I stalled for another few weeks, eventually settling on a Monday. The weekend dragged on endlessly. I showed up early Monday, anxious but ready to go. The clock ticked past 9 a.m., then 9:30 a.m., then 10 a.m., and the employee didn't show. She eventually called and said she had gotten caught up at an Amway convention over the weekend and wouldn't be in the office until Tuesday.

A day later, I was ready to go again. When she walked into the office, I said I wanted to chat. A few minutes later, I sat down with her and nervously said, "Things aren't working out." She looked at me, got up, took her purse, and left the office. She knew things weren't working, but she waited for us to fire her rather than quit.

I've learned that firing someone is always challenging, but it doesn't have to be the end of the relationship. In business, things often don't work out. When I fire someone, I like to give them the option of maintaining a relationship with me or ending it. I approach this optimistically, saying our relationship going forward is their choice. If they never want to talk to me again, I understand. If they want to remain friends, I'd be happy to. Some have chosen never to speak to me again. Others have remained close friends and, in a few cases, we've even had other business experiences together.

Provide Specific Actionable Advice

There's a tenuous balance between telling someone what to do and giving advice. This balance is difficult for a mentor, especially if you've previously been a CEO and are used to being "the decider."

As a mentor, you aren't the decider, but the CEO you mentor is. This dynamic is also true for many board-CEO relationships, where the board wants the CEO to make the ultimate decision.

While nice in theory, it's difficult in practice. One of my strengths is telling stories to illustrate a point, but one of my weaknesses is that my stories are often too long.

Remember the story about Bart Lorang at FullContact a few chapters ago? Bart was looking for specific, actionable advice. I was telling stories. If Bart had spent enough time processing my stories, he could have come up with the answer I was trying to guide him to. Or, he might draw the wrong inference and decide to do something different from what the stories were hinting. I expect Bart knew that but had trouble processing the stories in real time. Fortunately, in this situation, he was self-aware enough to ask for specific, actionable advice when needed.

Telling stories to illustrate something is powerful, but your mentee often seeks this specific, actionable advice. They aren't looking for you to tell them what to do, and you have to be comfortable with them ignoring your advice and doing something else. But pay attention to what your mentee needs, and when they need advice, give it.

Shifting the Decision Burden

As a mentor, avoid letting the decision burden shift to you. Since your mentee is the one who has to live with the decision, they should also be the one who makes the decision.

When you feel the decision burden shifting, pause. Be explicit with your mentee about the decision being contemplated. Ensure they interpret your feedback as data, not as a decision. Reiterate that this is their decision, not yours. And, if they make a decision that you disagree with, remember to support them.

Negotiating as Peers

When we raised our first Foundry fund, my founding partners and I established that we were all equal. Of the five of us, I had the most experience, and until we started Foundry, two of my partners had been working for me. But, we wanted to create an equal partnership from the beginning.

There was one exception. I thought I should get more carry in our first fund. However, I didn't have a preconceived notion of what that should be. I also was comfortable setting up a dynamic I learned from another VC, where we earned additional economics over time based on our contribution to the firm.

For our first fund, we decided to allocate 33 percent of the carry upfront but then have annual 360 reviews and allocate an additional 10 percent each year for the next six years based on our collective view of individual performance. Because this was complicated, we used an outside facilitator to help us through these interactions. This process forced us to discuss challenging issues in the partnership early, as the annual discussion to allocate additional economics generated truthful conversations.

My partners agreed I should have more carry and asked me what I wanted. I told them that while I had a number in mind, I wanted them to discuss it and decide. Then, I would accept whatever they came up with.

I viewed this as negotiating as peers. While I could have given advice or made a request, I wanted them to determine what they thought was fair and provide me with specific guidance.

Several days later, they proposed how to split up the 33 percent. I told them that it worked for me. They wanted to hear what I had in mind. I said it wasn't relevant. They pushed me on it. I told them I would only tell them if they accepted that the decision was theirs and that we wouldn't change it. They agreed. My number for myself was larger than theirs, and after I told them, they asked if I was okay with what they had proposed. I reminded them it was what they had decided, and I was good with it.

Shortly after raising our second fund, we decided to eliminate our complex year-end process and allocate carry equally. Our initial approach had served its purpose.

Be Challenging/Robust but Never Destructive

As a mentor, you'll often sense a founder isn't following your lead. You may be giving specific, actionable advice, but they aren't listening to you or understanding what you are saying. So, you become more direct. You push harder and more forcefully because you think it's important. But the founder still doesn't hear or understand.

Suddenly, you are irritated. You shut down and end the meeting. Or, you push harder. After the meeting, you vent to whoever will listen that this company is in real trouble because the founder isn't listening to you. Suddenly, you have become destructive to the founder and the company. You are no longer an effective mentor and are now being judgmental.

If you let this state persist, your frustration will continue to leak out to others and become destructive. You might say something negative to a potential investor, which means you've now affected the company's ability to raise capital. Talking trash about the founder to potential employees, customers, or business partners affects relationships. And, if you vent to a founder at another company, you hurt your reputation as a mentor.

Being a great mentor means being dedicated to helping founders build great companies. You should be clear and forceful in your words to ensure founders hear you. But when you leave the room, flip the switch and remain dedicated to helping the founders succeed, regardless of whether you think they listened to what you said.

Single-Turn vs. Multi-Turn Games

Entrepreneurship is a multi-turn game with multiple players over a long period. Behavior in a multi-turn game is different than in a single-turn game, as you can't optimize for the single turn and have to play with a long-term view. This approach is particularly true for your reputation as a mentor and investor.

Playing a multi-turn game is crucial with early-stage founders. As a mentor, your goal is to help founders succeed. Some people feel this can conflict with their goal as an investor, which is to have financially successful investments. While the conflict is valid if you approach entrepreneurship and investing as a single-turn game, the concepts are wholly aligned if you view it as a multi-turn game.

Here's a scenario: A company raises $2m of seed money from angel investors in a convertible note with a $6m cap. Assuming in the future that the company raises equity at or above that cap, the total dilution before the new money is 33 percent (equivalent to an equity financing of $2m at a $6m post-money valuation). The founders own 67 percent of the company, and the angel investors own 33 percent.

The company spends $2m building and launching its first product. The first release is underwhelming, but the company aggressively iterates, with feedback and support from its angel investors. The product gets much better. The company tries to raise a Series A, but there are no takers, and several prospects tell it, "Come back when you've made more progress with customers."

The company is running out of money. One of the angel investors, who happens to be a VC firm, decides to invest another $500,000 in the company. But instead of adding it to the note or doing an equity round with a price that could still be early-stage but below the cap, the VC firm argues that since the company couldn't raise a round, it is worthless.

The VC firm issues a term sheet to recapitalize the company. The term sheet converts all the convertible debt into a post-money valuation of $100k, essentially making the convertible debt worthless. The new money comes in at a pre-money valuation of $100k but includes a complete refresh of founder equity to 40 percent of the company. So the new investment gets 60 percent, the founders get 39.9 percent, and the $2m of seed money gets 0.1 percent.

As part of this, all seed investors can participate pro rata in the round to preserve their ownership percentage. However, the VC who drove the recap will control this equity round.

While this happens in entrepreneurship, it is usually limited to later rounds when a company is worth far less than the capital invested in it. For the company to survive, the only source of capital is from existing investors, many of whom are unwilling to participate. An insider uses a pay-to-play and a low valuation to reset the preferences and the cap table. The founders usually get wiped out completely, but existing management usually has new options for between 10 percent and 20 percent of the company. It's not pretty, but it happens.

But this is highly unusual in a seed round, as the company hasn't raised much money yet. Early-stage VCs play multi-turn games with one another and are hesitant to wipe one another out in early rounds. The valuations are generally low enough that adding incremental capital to a financing is viewed as adding on rather than recapitalizing the company.

In the described situation, neither the founders (getting re-upped to 40 percent) nor the VC respect the other angel investors. They are playing a single-turn game and only optimizing for themselves.

If this were a single-turn game, this might be rational. However, since entrepreneurship is a multi-turn game, the founders and the VC have damaged their reputations with angel investors. Since angel investors regularly interact and co-invest with other angel investors and seed VCs, they are unlikely to work with this VC again.

By playing a single-turn game, the VC is being shortsighted.

The Cliché of Disagree and Commit

While often attributed to Jeff Bezos and Amazon, the idea of disagreeing and committing goes back to the leadership principles of Andy Grove of Intel.

It can be difficult to disagree with your boss. Or a mentor. Or someone in a one-up position to you. It's also hard to commit to something with which you fundamentally disagree.

When used correctly, disagree and commit means arguing when the issue is up for debate. But, once you decide, you must support the decision entirely. When misused, it can be a tool for bludgeoning people, sowing dissent, undermining leaders, and talking trash behind the back of someone you disagree with.

Remember Gearbox, the Techstars company I discussed when discussing adopting at least one company? When I invested and joined the board, the founders, Ian Bernstein and Adam Wilson, added Paul Berberian as the third co-founder and CEO. They changed their name to Orbotix and then to Sphero, shipped a product, and made steady progress as a business.

Fundraising was extremely difficult for Sphero. While the product, a robotic ball controlled by a smartphone, was incredibly cool and technically challenging, prospective investors simply didn't see any meaningful market opportunity for it.

At some point, Paul began to be frustrated with the company's pace. His frustration coincided with Techstars partnering with Disney to create the Disney Accelerator. Paul, Ian, and Adam got excited about participating in a second Techstars accelerator with Disney.

Several board members, including me, were skeptical about the idea of a second accelerator, especially given that Sphero was a decent-sized company at this point and going through the accelerator would consume all of Paul, Ian, and Adam's attention for 90 days. But Paul, Ian, and Adam wanted to do it and advocated heavily for it. The board eventually supported it, and we committed to it fully. We decided the downside would be a three-month distraction and a cost of 7 percent dilution. We didn't know the upside but were willing to bet on it.

Bob Iger was one of the mentors for the Sphero team. Midway through the program, he showed the team a short video of the new *Star Wars* robot BB-8, which would have a lead role in the movie. He asked if the Sphero team could turn the Sphero robotic ball into a BB-8. Within 24 hours, Sphero had a prototype of it working. BB-8 became Sphero's next product, and when *The Force Awakens* came out, Sphero's BB-8 robot was a massive hit. Sphero's revenue grew from $15m to $150m that year, and the company was profitable. The commitment to the Disney Accelerator paid off in ways we couldn't envision.

Sphero then overcommitted to Disney with several other products, including the Ultimate Lightning McQueen,[26] which almost killed Sphero. But that's a story for another day.

---

26 An awesome, but also awesomely expensive, RC car.

Have Empathy. Remember That Startups Are Hard

Most founders encounter imposter syndrome at some point. Empathy is your most valuable tool when you notice a founder is struggling with it.

Imagine Mary, a young CEO, managing someone a decade her senior who is successful and highly skilled but prefers to work autonomously. This executive has a personal relationship with a board member who helped recruit them. They regularly do things outside their remit and communicate directly with a board member without including Mary.

While the executive has a notable impact, Mary becomes concerned about the executive's relationship with the board member. Imposter syndrome starts creeping in. Mary starts acting erratically with the executive, trying to control things while feeling anxious and beginning to worry that everything will fall apart. Stress builds, and she starts to have an existential crisis.

Listening to Mary describe the situation, your heart beats faster as you realize that Mary is experiencing something you once went through and learned from.

Try to put yourself in Mary's shoes. Feel her fear and anxiety. Do not try to fix her problem. When you recognize that Mary has imposter syndrome, slowly tell her a story about your past when you had imposter syndrome. Sink deeper into her anxiety. Explain how difficult the situation was for you. Let her relate to your past situation as you relate to her current situation.

At the moment, Mary needs someone she can talk to openly and transparently about what she is feeling. By being empathetic, telling your own story, and relating to her story, you are setting up a situation where she can talk to you more while listening to what you learned from your own experience.

Know when to suspend or defer your advice or judgment. The founder you are mentoring may not be able to hear your solution. However, they will probably feel your empathy, especially if you relate to their struggle.

Redefining the Goals

Part of empathy is realizing you don't know your mentee's goal. While they might express a goal, what they say is often a reaction to their stress. They want their anxiety to disappear, so they devise a solution, even if the answer is terrible. They just want the stress to end.

Use empathy to listen to the mentee to help get them out of distress. Working together, step back, reevaluate the situation, and intentionally explore the problem emotionally and functionally. Relate to the situation as though it were your own. Go slow and let your mentee hear that you are listening to and understanding their issue rather than just solving the problem or giving them advice.

At some point, you can start exploring the goal again.

It's Never Enough. Until It Is.

Amy and I spent a long weekend with friends in the Bay Area at their beautiful new house many years ago. The husband, whom I'll call

Marcus, had made about five million dollars when his first company went public and was now CEO of another startup.

Marcus was a few years older than us, worked 80 hours a week, and traveled constantly. He had two kids, and on this particular visit, I spent an entire day teaching his young son how to play *Doom*. "More chainsaw" echoed from the computer area, at least when I was around.

After dinner, the conversation shifted to work and money. After we both whined about continually being on the road, Marcus said, "I'll be all set after I make another five million dollars at this new company."

Being someone who at the time had less than five million dollars, I asked, "Before or after tax?"

Several years later, that company went public, and Marcus now had more than 10 million dollars. He was also the CEO of another company. Once again, we enjoyed an evening somewhere, and our conversation turned to money.

"I'll be all set after I make another 20 million dollars," said Marcus.

Being a smartass, I said, "What happened to being all set after five million more dollars, after tax?"

Marcus said, "Well, I want a few more things that I just need a little more money for."

Several years later, more money appeared in Marcus's bank account due to his extraordinary talents. He was CEO of yet another company, working over 80 hours a week and traveling constantly.

And then, one day, Marcus had a near-death accident.

A year later, Marcus retired.

Well, sort of. Marcus became a full-time angel investor. Now, he could spend time with his family, including his children, who were just becoming teenagers.

Marcus shifted all his energy to living his life rather than just making more money. Not surprisingly, he has been a successful angel investor, but he never again discussed needing more money.

PART 3

NAVIGATING GIVE FIRST

The Downside

Give First is not all rainbows and unicorns. It can be exhausting, burn you out, and damage your network.

Adam Grant, in *Give and Take: Why Helping Others Drives Our Success*, explains how reciprocity and success are linked and how helping others drives one's success. However, he also explains that seeing the impact you create is essential.[27]

If you find yourself giving to people who are takers, who don't contribute back to the community, and who aren't leaders and doers, you may find yourself becoming cynical about Give First. Or, you may ultimately say, "Fuck this whole Give First thing. I just give and give and give and give into an empty void and I'm burned out on it."

In the following sections, I'll discuss approaches I have used to overcome Give First's negative aspects. Some of these are tactical and easy to implement, while others have been difficult lessons to learn.

It took me a long time to understand how my behavior was causing episodic exhaustion. Continually giving first was part of this. And, it took me an even longer time to realize that this episodic exhaustion wasn't just simple fatigue but was often a contributor to a depressive cycle that I would end up in. While navigating these cycles, I couldn't modify my behavior until I understood the root cause. Only then was Give First sustainable without the adverse side effects.

---

27 Adam Grant. *Give and Take: Why Helping Others Drives Our Success.* Penguin Books, 2013.

Filters

The concept of networking is the opposite of Give First. I now consider networking "Ask First," and it is one of the worst ways to get a busy person's attention.

After a few experiments, I devised an approach to separating leaders from doers and everyone else. I initially applied this approach to the Boulder startup community but quickly realized it was helpful for all the random inbound inquiries I get. While I want to spend time with the leaders and support the doers, I don't want to spend in-person time figuring out who is a leader or a doer.

The trick to identifying leaders is to give people assignments.

Here's how it works. The type of inquiry I get varies and comes from people with different degrees of experience. My assignments also vary, but they address what the person is asking for while generating a result that will interest me.

Assume I get the following email: "Brad, I'm new to Boulder and very excited about getting involved in the startup community. I moved here from New York and have a deep background in DevOps. I have been a founder and meditate regularly. I'd love to meet for coffee to see how I can get involved in Boulder's startup scene. My resume is attached."

The assignment I give the person takes less than 30 minutes to complete and requires no specific knowledge on their part. For example:

"Welcome to Boulder. Unfortunately, I don't have time for coffee in the next few weeks, but I'd be happy to connect you with some of the local founders who might be relevant to you. Can you look through our portfolio on our website at foundry.vc and tell me who you'd like to be introduced to?"

At least half of the people don't respond, immediately reducing my workload and filtering out people who don't follow through.

Most of the rest send emails like, "I looked at your website and am very interested in StackHawk and Techstars. My last company had many API security issues, so I know the problem StackHawk is addressing. I also have experience mentoring founders, so I'd like to determine if I can join Techstars."

This person is a doer. I'll introduce them to the CEOs of StackHawk and Techstars. I use a double-opt-in approach: I send the thread to the person I want to introduce them to and ask permission to make the introduction. Assuming a positive response, I connect the doer, plugging them into the Boulder startup community and my world.

Now and then, I get a fantastic email.

"Brad, thanks for pushing me to be more precise. I realized I didn't need you to make the intro, so I've met with Joni Klippert at StackHawk and David Cohen at Techstars. There is a nice fit with Joni's company, and we are exploring a way to work together. David explained that there was a very long waiting list of mentors for the next program, so the most effective thing I could do was find one of the older Techstars companies and help them out. I'm already talking to the team from Sphero. Given my previous network management company experience, I contacted a founder at JumpCloud. I hope you don't mind if I write periodically and follow up on my progress."

This person is a leader. They went out and made things happen that positively impacted my world and theirs without needing additional help. They didn't ask me for more but offered plenty, making me want to do more for them. So, I'll respond with "Awesome. Welcome to town. Email me anytime about anything."

Obligatory Behavior

Give First is entirely optional—there is no obligatory behavior.

I've been on the receiving end of people telling me that I'm not "giving first." In many of these situations, they ask me for something and misinterpret Give First by assuming they can ask for what they want me to give them and that I'm somehow obligated to do this.

For a while, this made me frustrated. I felt attacked, especially when the other person increased the pressure while I tried to explain why they were misinterpreting Give First. In several instances, the other person got angry at me. And, more than once, someone told me that I and Give First was full of shit.

I eventually realized this was another situation where I needed to apply a filter. I didn't require people to interact with me using Give First. I view it as a philosophy and entirely optional. While I hoped it would appeal to people and watched it become broadly incorporated into the cultural fabric of Techstars, I knew that many people wouldn't get it, wouldn't like it, or simply didn't care.

When I encountered someone asserting that I had an obligation to them to Give First, I tried to explain why they were wrong. But I didn't invest any emotional energy in it, as I knew they would likely either get it or not. If they got it, great. If they didn't, that was also okay.

Boundaries

Do you identify with the person who said, "Fuck this whole Give First thing. I just give and give and give and give into an empty void and I'm burned out on it." Or do you feel a profound imbalance between giving and what you are getting back?

For the first 20 years of my adult life, I had difficulty setting boundaries between work and the rest of my life. This challenge contributed to the failure of my first marriage in my early twenties and almost caused the failure of my marriage to Amy.

Fortunately, Amy helped me understand the need and value of boundaries, and I started learning how to set them productively. It has taken me a long time to master this.

Give First is a "default yes" activity. When someone asks for help or offers a new opportunity, you default to saying yes. While you don't always say yes, you consider the situation and decide what to do. You regularly say yes in a "default yes" posture, especially to non-transactional requests where you don't know your ultimate reward.

I generally live this way and find it extremely powerful, satisfying, and fun. However, it's easy to overcommit and become overwhelmed. Shifting to "default no" can help establish boundaries when this happens. While your answer won't be an automatic no, you now have to consider if you can take on something else.

Another boundary-setting tactic is viewing Give First as part of your job. As a VC, this is easy for me since my job is to take a box of money that my investors give me and, over time, send them back a bigger box with more money. As long as it is legal and allowed under our investment agreements, how I do this is up to me. I've long believed that the returns that accrue using a Give First philosophy are much greater than those I'd see if I didn't. So, Give First is simply part of my job.

Recasting your job so that you can see the long-term benefits of Give First to your work can be applied to any role. It's particularly powerful when you want to be involved in your local startup community. Many companies have teams of people who work with startups and spend time and energy helping their local startup communities. They give away product, time, and expertise to get startups to use their company as part of the startup infrastructure. This behavior is no different than a traditional business development function. Still, the hyperlocal focus, especially around individual team members, actively engages with the local startup community. This engagement has a further positive impact, since the participants now also have a platform (their company) for participating in that community.

You can incorporate this idea if you are a founder of a startup. You have a very full-time job as a founder. As your company grows, your ability, and often desire, to spend time with the startup community diminishes. When I hear this from founders, I encourage them to be selfish. Instead of just giving anything to the startup community, they should think about what could help their startup. Do they need mobile developers? If so, host a monthly meetup for all the mobile developers in town. If fundraising is at the forefront of their mind, organize a dinner with other founders to discuss different approaches to raising capital.

If you approach Give First as part of your job, you'll naturally set boundaries for yourself.

Burnout

I've openly talked about several major depressive episodes that I've had.[28] Each of these depressive episodes lasted at least six months.

About a decade ago, I realized I had a similar emotion cycle every year for between 30 and 90 days between mid-October and mid-January. While I had been describing it as burnout from being exhausted from my efforts over the year, I finally acknowledged this was a shorter depressive episode. I realized I was both physically and psychologically exhausted and as winter began, I didn't have the reserves to prevent a depressive episode.

It doesn't matter whether you call this depression, burnout, or something else. Operating with a Give First philosophy can be cumulatively exhausting, especially if you don't set boundaries or have effective filters. For many years, I had neither, hence my end-of-year collapse.

Some of the things that Amy and I implemented in 2001, when our marriage almost failed, have helped. We started taking a week of vacation off the grid every quarter, and I started taking a digital sabbath, being completely offline on Saturdays. But it wasn't until I stopped telling myself a story about how I was just tired at the end of the year and didn't like the holiday season that I was able to face the fact that I was burned out and depressed.

---

28 For a detailed explanation, watch the interview I did with NOCD: "Mental Health in Entrepreneurship: Brad Feld on OCD and Depression," NOCD, August 8, 2024, https://www.youtube.com/watch?v=QydBkPO1sk8.

A decade of therapy that started during my last major depressive episode in 2013 and ended recently helped me modify a bunch of my historical behavior norms that were inhibiting my ability to sustain my energy over long periods without burning out. While some of this was tactical, like stopping drinking alcohol, going to sleep earlier, not using an alarm clock to wake up, and meditating regularly, the real change came from better understanding myself.

Many good and bad things happened during this decade of therapy. As I gradually understood myself better and got to the roots of some of my unproductive, dysfunctional, or challenging behaviors, I learned ways to change my behavior so I wouldn't burn out.

This exploration is deeply personal. While I don't have the answer for anyone else, I firmly believe that therapy or coaching can help you understand what is happening, what matters, and how to sustain your energy over a long, productive period.

Give First, Finish Last?

Keith Coleman of Fraudmarc emailed David Cohen and me with the subject "give first, finish last." In it, he explained his reservations about Give First. He asked, "Is Give First right for new founders focused on their company's survival? Or is Give First for people who have already met with success and who have the time and resources to be able to give?"

After some discussion, David and I decided to do a Give First podcast with Keith on this topic.[29]

Keith recognized the benefits of Give First and joined other founders in making the Pledge 1% commitment to the Techstars Foundation. Keith explained how Fraudmarc's Pledge 1% commitment was powerful. It meant something and created stronger personal connections within the Techstars universe, resulting in others prioritizing his calls and requests for help. It also helped Keith shape the cultural norms of his company.

Are those benefits—including the knowledge that there are people with both an ability and a desire to help guide you in some future moment when you may need it—tangible and quantitative? Maybe. But, if you've absorbed the concept of Give First, you know it often isn't, especially at the moment when you Give First.

---

29 "Fraudmarc's Keith Coleman on the Value of Give First as a Founder," Techstars, September 21, 2021, https://www.techstars.com/blog/podcasts/fraudmarcs-keith-coleman-on-the-value-of-give-first-as-a-founder.

In the end, Keith suggested encouraging founders to embrace Give First. But, he thought we should be more precise that on a philanthropic level, especially financially, founders who have had success can do it at a different level than founders who are just starting. While this may seem obvious, our conversation with Keith showed that we weren't emphasizing this clearly and that founders will respond to Give First differently depending on where they are in their journey.

What Is Entrepreneurial Tzedakah?

As we wrap up, I want to link Give First to the idea of giving back philanthropically when you are successful. Many people contributed to your success, and by giving back to your community, you can improve the place you live while helping perpetuate the next generation of founders.

For many years, I searched for a word that embodied entrepreneurial philanthropy. Amy and I were early participants in the Social Venture Partners initiative, which applied entrepreneurial thinking to philanthropy (Amy co-founded the Social Venture Partners chapter in Boulder). One of our Anchor Point Foundation initiatives is Entrepreneurship, and we've funded many different programs over the last 30 years.

Eventually, I settled on tzedakah (צדקה), a delicious Hebrew word that means "righteousness" but is often translated to mean "charity." It is directly related to the Eight Levels of Charitable Giving that the Sephardic Jewish philosopher Maimonides devised in the Middle Ages.

The Eight Levels of
Charitable Giving

While I don't judge people on their charitable activity or how they do it, it's worth considering Maimonides's framework. The levels, in descending order, with the most potent listed first, are:

Giving an interest-free loan, forming a partnership, giving a grant, or finding a job for a person so that the person no longer lives by relying upon others.

Giving tzedakah anonymously to an unknown recipient via a person or public fund that is trustworthy.

Giving tzedakah anonymously to a known recipient.

Giving tzedakah publicly to an unknown recipient.

Giving tzedakah before being asked.

Giving adequately after being asked.

Giving willingly but inadequately.

Giving in sadness or out of pity.

Angel Investing as For-Profit Philanthropy

When I saw Maimonides's Eight Levels of Charitable Giving for the first time, I said to Amy, "Angel investing is the first Maimonides level!" She looked at me like I was speaking Martian or playing some new video game.

I made my first angel investment in 1994 into a company called NetGenesis with money from selling my first company. The list of people from that company I've worked with on multiple companies includes Will Herman, Rajat Bhargava, Matt Cutler, Niel Robertson, Sean O'Sullivan, and Terry Duryea. And to this day, Will and Rajat are two of my closest friends.

When I made that investment, I hoped for a positive return. However, I was only thinking about the financial aspect at the time. While the financial return was meaningful (NetGenesis went public in 1999), the non-financial return was much more significant for me and many others.

At the first Techstars demo day at CU Boulder's campus in 2007, I got up on stage and, after saying appreciative words to all the founders and mentors, I told the mentors and the investors attending that there was one thing they could do that day that would have a profound impact on all the founders in the room.

"Write a check and invest in at least one company. It doesn't matter what size of check you write. Whatever you are comfortable with. But pick at least one company and fund them. Commit today. Think of it as for-profit philanthropy. In your worst case, you get a tax deduction, just like a charitable donation. In your best case, you'll make a bunch of money that you can then invest in other startups."

That was the first time I connected angel investing to for-profit philanthropy, and it feels like an ideal approach to Entrepreneurial Tzedakah.

Pledge 1%

While numerous initiatives have created a way for founders and their companies to contribute philanthropically when successful, my favorite is Pledge 1%.

The long path to its current state began when Ryan Martens, the co-founder and CTO of Rally Software, told me he wanted to do something similar to what Marc Benioff had done with the Salesforce Foundation. In 1999, Salesforce created a foundation and gave it 1 percent of its equity before going public. Ryan had met Suzanne DiBianca, one of the foundation's co-founders, and subsequently learned about the Entrepreneurs Foundation and the Bay Area chapter.

Ryan and I co-founded the Entrepreneurs Foundation of Colorado in 2007. Over 100 companies joined, including Rally, Foundry, and Techstars. We based it on what Salesforce had done, where the idea was to contribute 1 percent of the company's equity, time, product, or profit back to its community. Over $10 million has been returned to the Colorado community due to equity contributions from the member companies.

After a few years, my partner Seth Levine joined the Entrepreneurs Foundation of Colorado board, and Seth, Ryan, and a few others decided to take the idea nationwide. They coordinated with many leaders, including several in the Bay Area, to co-found Pledge 1%. It was a natural evolution from what we had been doing at the Entrepreneurs

Foundation—perhaps even a revolution if you look at what Pledge 1% has been able to accomplish since its founding.

Pledge 1% has become incredibly sophisticated in its approach, including numerous playbooks for companies at different stages. It has also expanded how companies and individuals can participate. Today, Pledge 1% has over 19,000 members globally and has helped companies contribute nearly $3 billion to their communities.

Techstars Foundation

We created the Techstars Foundation in 2015 to make innovation and entrepreneurship more accessible and inclusive. Around that time, we saw many organizations talking about diversity and inclusion. We didn't think that talk was enough, so we wanted to put our money and energy toward this problem. So, we thought about our superpower. As for-profit investors, we succeeded by identifying very early-stage organizations that could scale and have outsized impact over time. We thought it made sense to think about nonprofits in the same way. We'd find and support them early before anyone else knew they existed. We'd work to surround them with talent from our network of mentors, investors, and founders and try to help them succeed. We'd be the seed investor for potentially scalable nonprofits attempting to tackle the problem of diversity and inclusion in tech.

The funding came from Techstars founders, board members, employees, mentors, alums, and several exits of companies that had contributed equity to the Techstars Foundation. Many Techstars companies pledged equity to the Techstars Foundation and other nonprofit organizations. Techstars provided staffing for the Techstars Foundation so that we could ensure that nearly 100 percent of the donations went to nonprofits instead of salaries.

We always believed that while money could help nonprofits, the Techstars global network could help even more. One of our goals was to promote our grants in our newsletters and social media to encourage more people to contribute money or effort to help these nonprofits succeed.

The Techstars Foundation has made over $2.3 million in grants to over 50 organizations. In addition to funding the organizations, we elevated and exposed them to the extended Techstars network. When people were interested, we played matchmaker and got them involved.

Afterword

I have been developing, writing, and sharing my thoughts about the Give First philosophy for over 15 years. During this time, I have mentored thousands of founders and invested in hundreds of companies. I have made plenty of mistakes and learned an incredible amount.

The Give First philosophy is a guiding principle in my life. It has allowed me to build deep relationships, create successful businesses, and positively impact the world. It's not just about giving; it's about building authentic connections, fostering trust, and empowering others to succeed. These are also cornerstones of effective mentorship, which I've tried to illustrate throughout the book.

Give First has become a way of life. It defines my values and explains the kind of person I want to be in the world. The benefits of embracing the Give First philosophy have been extraordinary, and anyone can adopt this philosophy and experience similar benefits.

I hope this book has inspired you to explore how Give First could apply to your life. I strongly believe that giving without expectation of return is the most effective way to achieve many goals. So, go out there and Give First. The rest will follow.

Acknowledgments

David Cohen for coming up with the Techstars Mentor Manifesto. And Jon Bradford for providing early feedback.

Jay Batson for writing the original blog posts for Be Challenging/ Robust but Never Destructive and Have Empathy. Remember That Startups Are Hard.

Keith Coleman, for both giving first and challenging David Cohen and me on how early-stage founders can or cannot Give First.

Yoav Lurie, for sketching out his recollection of the Simple Energy story.

Matt Blumberg, David Brown, David Cohen, Ben Casnocha, Jerry Colonna, Nicole Glaros, Will Herman, Jaclyn Hester, Tom Higley, Dave Jilk, Elizabeth Kraus, Jenny Lawton, James Oliver, Eliot Peper, and Alex Rigopulos for their extensive feedback on the first draft I submitted to the publisher.

Seth Levine, Daniel Feld, and Phil Weiser for giving me even more extensive feedback on the second draft I submitted to the publisher after I shelved the book for a year.

Dov Seidman, for his book *How: Why How We Do Anything Means Everything . . . in Business (and in Life)*, and our many conversations around the topic.

Adam Grant, for his book *Give and Take: Why Helping Others Drives Our Success* and a memorable lunch we had together in Aspen one winter day.

Rohit Bhargava, Lynnette McCurdy, Megan Wheeler, Kameron Bryant-Sergejev, Christina Caruccio, Marnie McMahon, Allison Griffith, Jessica Angerstein, Athena Potkovic and their team at Ideapress Publishing for helping this book become a reality.

Early mentors of mine: Eugene Scott, Chris and Helena Aves, Charlie Feld, and Eric von Hippel.

Len Fassler and Jerry Poch for taking a flyer on me, changing the trajectory of my work, and teaching me so many things.

Ron Fisher for quietly being there in the background and helping guide me on many issues even when he didn't realize it.

Jana Matthews, for the many conversations we've had about entrepreneurship, and the many things I've learned working with her, going back over 30 years.

The thousands of mentors who have worked with Techstars companies over the past 18 years.

My mother, Cecelia Feld, and my father, Stanley Feld, whose parenting often contained elements of mentorship.

Amy Batchelor, for being my editor, life partner, food fairy, soulmate, and someone I want to always share time with.

About the Author

BRAD FELD has been an early-stage entrepreneur and investor since 1987. He co-founded two venture capital firms, Foundry Group and Mobius Venture Capital, and multiple companies, including Techstars. Brad is a writer and speaker on venture capital investing and entrepreneurship and has written several popular books, including *Venture Deals* and *Startup Communities*. He runs the Anchor Point Foundation with his wife, Amy Batchelor.

Other Books by the Author

Do More Faster: Techstars Lessons to Accelerate Your Startup (with David Cohen)

Venture Deals: Be Smarter Than Your Lawyer and Venture Capitalist (with Jason Mendelson)

Startup Communities: Building an Entrepreneurial Ecosystem in Your City

Startup Life: Surviving and Thriving in a Relationship with an Entrepreneur (with Amy Batchelor)

Startup Boards: A Field Guide to Building and Leading an Effective Board of Directors (with Mahendra Ramsinghani and Matt Blumberg)

Startup Opportunities: Know When to Quit Your Day Job (with Sean Wise)

The Startup Community Way: Evolving an Entrepreneurial Ecosystem (with Ian Hathaway)

The Entrepreneur's Weekly Nietzsche: A Book for Disruptors (with Dave Jilk)